True Word for tough times

True Word

for tough times

Dale Ralph Davis

 **BOOKS**

First published 2013

ISBN: 978-085234-934-2

Evangelical Movement of Wales

The EMW works in both Welsh and English and seeks to help Christians and churches by:

- running children's camps and family conferences
- providing theological training and events for ministers
- running Christian bookshops and a conference centre
- publishing magazines and books

Bryntirion Press is a ministry of EMW.

Past issues of EMW magazines and sermons preached at our conferences are available on our web site: www.emw.org.uk

Published by Bryntirion Press, Bryntirion, Bridgend CF31 4DX, Wales, in association with EP BOOKS, Faverdale North, Darlington, DL3 0PH, UK.

EP BOOKS are distributed in the USA by:
JPL Fulfillment, 3741 Linden Avenue Southeast, Grand Rapids, MI 49548.
E-mail: sales@jplfulfillment.com
Tel: 877.683.6935

Contents

		Page
Preface		7
1	Astounding Word (Jeremiah 1)	9
2	Can this prophet be saved? (Jeremiah 15:10-21)	27
3	The yoke is no joke (Jeremiah 27 - 29)	43
4	Jerusalem burning (Jeremiah 37 - 39)	61
5	Faithful futility, a pattern of ministry (Jeremiah 40 - 45)	79

Preface

The following pages contain messages given at the Aberystwyth Conference in August 2010. They have appeared in this printed form because Mrs Jennifer Eveson willingly endured the literary purgatory of turning recorded messages into written material. Huge thanks to her for both her skill and — undoubtedly — her anguish!

I have 'touched up' and clarified this written form at points, but all remains substantially as originally delivered. These expositions were preached (except the fifth, which was a lecture), and I have not smoothed out the preaching style; hence the frequent roughness and 'choppiness' of the prose. Translations of the biblical text are often my own. Occasionally I paraphrase parts of the text; these, I think, are readily recognizable.

There was no human motivation for choosing the prophecy of Jeremiah for these messages, except convenience and fascination. I happened to be working in Jeremiah at the time a decision had to be made about 'what to preach' at Aberystwyth. But I am also strangely fascinated by both Jeremiah's prophecy and his ministry. His was a ministry without perks and lacking conventional encouragements. I infer that grace must be real because Jeremiah endured to the end. That both fascinates and heartens me.

Of course, when one has to choose five passages to preach out of a long book like Jeremiah, one has to be selective. The sections I chose tend to focus on the 'negative' side of Jeremiah's ministry, his 'pulling up' and 'throwing down' work (cf. Jer. 1:10). Don't let that give you a skewed view of Jeremiah; remember that he had a 'building and planting' ministry as well. Note the way he preached 'a future and a hope' in chapters 30 - 33 (though that hope was not for his own contemporaries). However, I have focused on 'down' passages, partly because I think they supply a healthy corrective to some of the flippant and flimsy optimism we meet in certain 'Christian' propaganda about the Christian life and ministry. My prayer is that a number of the Lord's servants who are slogging on in the paths of righteousness will, by the Spirit's chemistry, be strangely comforted by this tormented prophet and the 'ruthless Warrior' who stood at his side.

Dale Ralph Davis
July 2013

1

Astounding Word

Jeremiah 1

As we begin to consider the book of Jeremiah, we note first of all that it is the longest prophetic book as regards content in the canon of Scripture. An initial reading might suggest a lack of coherence, as matters are not presented in precise chronological order. But there is more coherence than many critics might think.

Jeremiah began his ministry around 627 BC, when the LORD called him and so God's Word came to Jeremiah. You notice that there is no distinction made between the divine and the human word. The chapter opens with 'These are the words of Jeremiah' followed immediately by the statement that the Word of Yahweh came to him. Then you will notice in verse 9 that the Lord expresses it in Hebrew as 'My words in your mouth': a divine word, a human word — perhaps a mystery, but no conflict.

I do not know what the plumbing is like in the UK. One of the things we have in some of our bathrooms in the States is a little device called a shut-off valve. Once in a while, perhaps, because grandchildren love to stuff toilet tissue down the toilet, you may have had the experience of the toilet pan threatening to overflow. Well, under the toilet tank is that little shut-off valve, a little oval handle, and you just turn it clockwise: it shuts the water off within half an inch and you are safe. You generally do not think much about that shut-off valve — it is a very ordinary thing. You know it is there but you do not pay much attention to it — it is just part of the furniture. When you have to use it, you say, 'Well, that is brilliant! That is ingenious! That is wonderful!' Something may seem very ordinary and then it can suddenly strike you as being a marvellous affair.

I think sometimes the Word of God is like that in the church. There are times, sadly, when we regard the Word of God as rather ordinary. It has just been with us (thankfully); it is just there so we may not regard it as really quite astounding. But I think Jeremiah 1 is telling us that this is an astounding Word.

Why are we talking about the Word? Well, because it mentions in the text the call of the prophet. If it was the call of a philosopher we would be talking about arguments; if it was the call of a cook we would be talking about food; if it was the call of a mechanic we would be talking about tools; and if it was the call of a butcher we would be talking about meat. But it is the call of a prophet, so we talk about the Word of God. The point about the Word of God is that it really is an astounding Word. Why is the Word of God astounding? To answer the question let's examine the text in detail.

Relentless Word

First of all, the Word of God is astounding because it is so relentless. Verses 1-3 start off with a brief genealogy, geography and history, all of which may not interest you particularly. But you must notice the times.

Astounding Word

Yahweh's Word came in religious times

The Word of Yahweh came, first of all, in religious times — it came 'in the days of Josiah son of Amon king of Judah, in the thirteenth year of his reign [627 BC]'. This is when Jeremiah apparently began his public ministry — in the days of Josiah. What a marvellous time that was! In a way it came as a relief because, after half a century of almost complete paganism, especially in the reign of Manasseh, Josiah came to the throne and he instituted reform: reform of worship and sacraments, which also included a renewed commitment to Yahweh.

However, if you read Jeremiah 3:10, it seems that the reform under Josiah may have been rather superficial. It was an official overall kind of outward reform which may not have had much effect on the people. But it was far better than Manasseh's time. Yahweh's Word came in religious times.

Yahweh's Word came in hostile times

It kept on coming (v. 3): 'in the days of Jehoiakim, son of Josiah, king of Judah'. Jehoiakim was hostile, and had no qualms about getting rid of the prophets. In chapter 26 Uriah had prophesied like Jeremiah, and Jehoiakim did not like it. His intention was to seize Uriah and dispose of him; but Uriah fled to Egypt. However, Jehoiakim sent his 'Gestapo' to Egypt, brought him back and liquidated him. That is the way Jehoiakim dealt with messengers of the Word.

In chapter 36, a scroll that Baruch had transcribed at Jeremiah's dictation was being read to Jehoiakim. Some of his courtiers had already heard the scroll read and believed what it said, so they wanted this word, which consisted almost entirely of judgement, to be read to Jehoiakim because of the danger the country was in. It was winter and Jehoiakim was sitting before the fire in his quarters or his royal flat, and when Jehudi had read three or four columns of the scroll, Jehoiakim took his penknife, cut it off, flicked it into the fire and burned it up. That is what Jehoiakim thought about the Word of God. But the Word of Yahweh came in the days of Jehoiakim. They were hostile times, but the Word of Yahweh kept on coming.

Yahweh's Word came in nervous times

You notice in the middle of verse 3 that the word came until the completion of 'the eleventh year of Zedekiah, son of Josiah, king of Judah'. Zedekiah was the last king of Judah before the people were taken in the final wave of exile in 587 BC. Zedekiah is an interesting fellow. You read of him in Jeremiah 38. He was the kind of person who got up every morning and checked the papers and the ratings and the polls to see where he was. To Zedekiah no issue was so great that you could not flip-flop over it. He was always up and down, a 'yo-yo' king. But Yahweh's Word came in those times as well.

Yahweh's Word came in disastrous times

You notice that the end of verse 3 reads 'until the exile of Jerusalem in the fifth month' (that is, of the eleventh year of Zedekiah). The Word of Yahweh came in disastrous times when the Babylonians breached the city, when the other fortified cities of Judah were already taken, when they burned the temple, when they knocked down the walls and took the last wave of the people into exile.

The first part of verse 2 says that 'the Word of Yahweh came'. In verse 3 the verb form is a bit different and can be translated quite rightly, 'and it went on coming in the days of Jehoiakim'. It just went on 'coming'. In times of superficial religion (Josiah), of hardened indifference (Jehoiakim), in days of weak compromise (Zedekiah), in days of national disaster, the Word of God kept on coming. It is relentless; it is unstoppable; it simply keeps on coming, no matter what the climate seems to be, no matter what the circumstances are.

Isn't God kind? You see what these three almost boring verses in the first chapter of Jeremiah are teaching you? That Yahweh does not leave his people without direction even in the darkest of times. God's Word comes even in the days of Jehoiakim, when they destroy and ignore his Word. Is he not still kind to us? In a day when the church loves gimmicks and glitz and amplifiers, even in the so-called evangelical church where there does not seem to be much appetite for either the written Word or the preached Word, it is still here. The Word of Yahweh is so relentless and that is why it is so astounding.

Fragile Word

Secondly, the Word of God is astounding because it is so fragile. Look at verses 4-9 and particularly at verses 4-6. The word comes to Jeremiah individually; note verse 4, 'the word of Yahweh came to me'. Then in verse 5, among other things Yahweh said, 'I have appointed you a prophet to the nations.' Jeremiah knew that being a prophet means speaking the Word of God and he responds to the Lord in verse 6, 'Ah, Lord Yahweh, I do not know how to speak, for I am a youth.' The word 'youth' has the idea of inexperience; it is a flexible term. You have to go by the context as to how you understand it in terms of designating age; but he probably was not very old at all. However, the stress seems to be on the experiential barrier that Jeremiah feels — his lack of experience.

At the same time, there is a social barrier. John Mackay points this out in his commentary when he indicates that in such a culture people would be more likely to listen to older people. You have the wise elders and the people with some age and experience and these are the ones you approach for counsel and direction. But here is this slip of a youth, probably a teenager, and Yahweh has called him to speak his Word. Who is going to listen to a youngster like that? You begin to realize that he has no social clout and yet God calls him to be a prophet.

We have to ask why God keeps doing this. We have seen it before. Why does God seem to sabotage his own programme by the way he carries it out? Why does he do that? It seems to be a practice he has been carrying on for some time. Why did he take a pagan idolater who could not have children and use him to establish his people in this world? You remember that that is true of Abraham. You remember Joshua 24:2-3. Abraham was not someone who was looking for new light. No, Joshua said that Abraham and Nahor and their father, Terah, served other gods beyond the river. Abraham was a pagan. Then we have these marvellous words in Joshua 24:3: 'Then I took your father Abraham'. He took a man and his wife Sarai — and in Genesis 11:30 he said that Sarai was barren; she had no child. And that fact hangs like a shadow over ten or eleven chapters of Genesis, as the promise about many descendants looks as if it will never come to pass. Will there ever be a people of God in this world? Why does God work that way? He calls a pagan idolater who cannot have children and then later he calls a devious schemer like Jacob who can.

Then you have an eighty-year-old failure who seems to have lost his vision for the deliverance of his people when you read about Moses in Exodus. It makes us wonder. You notice that he calls Jephthah, an illegitimate freebooter who is despised and rejected by men, to work a partial deliverance for his people (Judg. 11). Why does he have dealings with people like that? But this is a pattern. He takes the youngest child of a family of seven or eight sons, who was not even thought important enough to invite to the king's selection ceremony and dinner (1 Sam. 16). So you have David.

Why does Yahweh do that? Why does God keep using people like this who always seem to have some defect or deficiency? It almost makes you say, 'OK. What kind of loser is the Lord going to call this time?'

It happens sometimes in history. For example, there was a president in the United States by the name of John Tyler. I think he was the tenth president. He was actually vice-president and at home in Williamsburg, Virginia, when he received word that the president, William Henry Harrison, had died. Harrison had been unwise, reading out his two-hour-long inauguration address in bitterly cold weather without being suitably attired. He fell ill and died within a month. So much for long sermons!! But sadly, unlike many presidents who were well off financially, Tyler was not wealthy at all. He didn't even have the money to make the trip to Washington. So his friends clubbed together and loaned him the money so that he could attend his own inauguration. That is just not very presidential; it does not fit the mould.

It is a similar situation in Jeremiah. Why does God follow this practice? Why does he take such fragile, weak, in some way disqualified people for his service? In Jeremiah's case, though, this is a step that God took long ago. You notice in verse 5, 'Before I formed you in the belly I knew you and before you came forth from the womb I had set you apart and appointed you a prophet to the nations.' This happened before Jeremiah was even conceived. So what matters is not Jeremiah's competence or qualifications particularly, but rather God's decision. It all rests on that.

You might wonder what this has to do with us. We are not prophets. Certainly, I am not a prophet. You might claim to be one. I am not.

So in one sense, what is particularly true of Jeremiah here does not apply to me or to you. What has this got to do with us? There is a sense, however, in which we face an analogous situation. It is in Romans 8:28-29, especially verse 28: '...but we know that to those who love God, all things work together for good, to those who are called according to his purpose. Because whom he foreknew, he also marked out beforehand to be shaped to the likeness of his Son.' It is important to keep verse 28 in mind, when it says, 'All things work together for good.' It is important to understand that verse 29 indicates what that 'good' is. What is the good that all things work together towards? The good is being shaped in the likeness of Jesus, according to verse 29. It is something broader than a particular call to be a prophet, but it is the same kind of thing. It is something that rests with God's decision and with God's determination. You might wonder as you look at that, what hope is there? Look at us! What hope is there of sin-ridden, hard-headed, psychologically twisted people like us being shaped in the likeness of God's Son?

But verse 29 explains. It is the same thing in one sense as Jeremiah. There is something that happened first. 'Because whom he foreknew'. And notice it does not say, 'whom he knew about'. He did not know *about* them, he knew *them*, and that knowing is not a distant knowing; it is the intimate knowing of the Bible. I think John Murray is right when he says in his commentary on Romans that in Romans 8:29 'foreknew' is essentially the same as fore-loved; whom he fore-loved he also marked out beforehand. In case you have an allergy to the 'p' word, 'predestined', 'marked out beforehand' is what it means.

So our being shaped in the likeness of Jesus his Son rests ultimately on the decision of God, it rests on his determination to bring it about. I know it does not exclude our efforts as we have to strive after holiness and so on. But when everything is said and done, it rests on him; it rests on God's decision. It is not because we are such promising material. It is not because of our faltering attempts. It is not as if the Lord looked upon us and said, 'That looks like a sanctification starter kit.' No, no!

So you come back to the main point. The Word of God is so astounding because the Word of God is so fragile. Just look at the servants he calls!

Dominating Word

Thirdly, the Word of God is astounding because the Word of God is so dominating. We notice in verse 5 that the Lord said to Jeremiah 'I have appointed you a prophet to the nations', and then he fleshes that out in verse 10: 'See, I have appointed you this day over the nations and over the kingdoms, to pull up and to pull down, to destroy and to throw down, to build and to plant.' Verse 10 is the key verse of the prophecy of Jeremiah. As you study the prophecy you will see those last six verbs coming up again and again: 'to pull up and to pull down, to destroy and to throw down, to build and to plant'.

So there is the key verse of the book. Verse 10 tells us what the prophet's mission is with the Word. Notice the emphasis on the infinitives. There are four that are negative and two that are positive. 'To pull up, to pull down, to destroy and to throw down' have the dominance, four negatives. The two positives are 'to build and to plant'. Notice the sequence — the negative comes before the positive. So there is an emphasis on the negative; there is an emphasis on judgement, not so much an emphasis on restoration. There is also a definite sequence — judgement comes before restoration. That seems to be the prophet's mission with the Word. So Jeremiah's dominant theme — and it does cause him problems — is a word and message of judgement.

Notice that you also see the prophet's position with the Word. The Lord says, 'See I have appointed you this day over the nations and over the kingdoms.' That is absolutely staggering. You see what he is saying. There is a certain royalty about the prophet Jeremiah. In one sense the prophet is king. He has been placed over the nations and over the kingdoms — that is his position. So whatever Yahweh says about a nation or a kingdom through Jeremiah will take place. You see that fleshed out in chapters 18 and 27.

We live in a culture that does not think this way. We are so secularized that even biblical people have a hard time thinking this way. We think that what determines the ruin or the prosperity of a nation are economic factors, political decisions, sociological shifts, technological advantages, military alignments, natural resources — all those sorts of things. But no, it is the divine decree. It is whatever word Yahweh speaks through his prophet regarding a nation or kingdom — that is what determines its welfare or its pain.

So Jeremiah in one sense is king, and the Lord says, 'he speaks my royal Word'; and whatever that Word declares about a nation will come to pass. 'I have appointed you this day over the nations and over the kingdoms.' Can you sense how ludicrous that seems? Think about it. 'I have set you, Jeremiah, a mere prophet, over nations and kingdoms.' How ludicrous that this obscure priest from a puny village should hold the direction of history and the fate of nations on the tip of his tongue. That is staggering. It is difficult to take in the full force of this. I have an illustration which may help.

In September 1680, Donald Cargill, one of the Scottish covenanters, was preaching on Ezekiel 21:25-27, where God says, 'Remove the diadem and take off the crown...' When Cargill's sermon was finished, he went on in well-weighed words (although some people think he was too rash) to excommunicate Charles Stuart, the King of England and Scotland; James, Duke of York; James, Duke of Monmouth; John, Duke of Lauderdale; John, Duke of Rothes; and a couple of others. He spelled out their sins in detail and announced them excommunicated from Christ's church. Of course, he paid for that. He was apprehended and executed at the end of July 1681. Interestingly enough, though, the very night before Cargill was executed for that act, the Duke of Rothes, one of the men he had excommunicated, was about to die. His life of intemperance had sapped his strength. As he lay on his deathbed, he called for some of his wife's ministers, because she was a Christian. So a couple of gospel ministers came to meet with the dying Duke of Rothes. They pointed him to the mercy of God in the Saviour Jesus Christ. But he could not believe that such mercy could be for him. Then he said, 'We all thought little of what Cargill did in excommunicating us; but I find that sentence binding upon me now, and it will bind to eternity.' And as Alexander Smellie says, 'The Duke of Rothes went out into the night.' It was said that Cargill did a rash thing, but there is something august and magnificent in the spectacle of a poor, ageing, hunted minister announcing the displeasure of high heaven against the powers and principalities that sway the destiny of a country. Of all the audacity! In a sense, a prophet being a king.

Well, that is what we have in Jeremiah. Of course, the world thinks that it is nonsense — the world's nations and politics subject to the will and the direction of the living God!! The BBC and CNN and Fox News do not think like that, and the parliaments and embassies of the world are not on that wavelength. They might say, in the usual idiom of our times, 'We are very offended by that. Please apologize.'

What God essentially says is: 'When you speak a word in my name about any nation or kingdom, I will bring that about.' It is really the same thing that is said to Israel in Deuteronomy 8:2-3, the very text that Jesus quoted in his temptations. In Deuteronomy 8:2-3 Moses says to Israel, 'You shall remember all the way in which Yahweh your God has led you these forty years in the wilderness in order that he might humble you, to test you to know what is in your heart, whether you will keep his commandments or not. So he humbled you and caused you to hunger and fed you with manna which you did not know, nor did your fathers know, in order that he might make you know that it is not by bread alone that man continues to live, but by everything that comes forth from the mouth of Yahweh that man goes on living.'

What is being said? It is not even really the manna in the wilderness that sustained Israel. God gave it to them. He humbled them by it. He showed them their destitution, that they were utterly dependent on it. But it is not by bread alone that man goes on living. What is it that causes him to go on living? Everything that comes out of the mouth of Yahweh — that is what causes him to go on living. And what is that? That is his daily decision to sustain his people. A situation reflecting Deuteronomy 8:3 would be something like this, if you can imagine it. A couple of Israelites early in the morning are going out to gather the manna. One sees the manna on the ground. He turns to the other and says, 'I see Yahweh has decided that we should live for another day.'

You see, everything that goes forth from the mouth of Yahweh is his decree and his decision. If he decrees and decides that Israel is going to live for another day, he will make sure that the manna is there. It is there because Yahweh decides that he will give it to them. It rests on everything that comes out of Yahweh's mouth. That is what decides everything.

This is how the Word of God is so dominating. I think Jeremiah 1:10 ought to be plastered above the entrance to the United Nations building, because it is what comes out of Yahweh's mouth that will make the difference as to whether a nation is to be buried or built, or whether a kingdom is to be raised up or ruined. The Word of God is so dominating.

Fanatical Word

But, fourthly, the Word of God is astounding because it is so fanatical. Look at verses 11-19. We do not have time to go into this in great detail, but I want to hit the high spot. In verses 11-12 the Lord is underscoring the certainty of his Word. He asks Jeremiah, 'What do you see?' and he says, 'I see a shoot of an almond tree: the shoot of a *shaqed* [*shaw-kayd*] is what I see.' And Yahweh says, 'You have seen well, for I am *shoqed(ing)* [*show-kay-ding*] over my Word to do it.' So there is a word-play, or a sound-play; the word for 'almond' conjures up the similar word for 'watching' and so stresses the certainty with which the Lord will watch over his Word and bring it to pass.

But then you notice the main focus is on the content of the Word in verses 13-16. The content of that Word comes by another vision. 'What do you see, Jeremiah?' 'Well, I see this pot [maybe a cooking pot of large proportions] — it's boiling and a bit unsteady. It's facing away from the north and it's going to spill all the scalding contents down on the southern part of the land. It's going to come upon Judah.' The idea is that the judgement is going to come from the north — the Lord is going to call all the clans of the kingdoms of the north, and this is probably at least a reference to the coming of the Babylonians and the destruction of Jerusalem.

Notice in verse 16 what Yahweh is going to do and why: 'And I shall declare my judgements with them for all their evil, because [this spells out their evil and it can be translated either 'in that' or 'because'] they have forsaken me and they have burned incense to other gods and bowed down to the works of their hands.'

That is a picture of what is coming and verse 16 (which I want to emphasize) is an indication of why it is coming. You see at the end of verse 16, 'They have forsaken me.' That is what Yahweh dwells on. That is what drives him to white heat. That is what disturbs him most. Some people may find that odd.

I remember some years ago hearing about some executive of a motel chain. They said to him, 'If you could get one word across to people, what would it be?' He said, 'It would be, "The shower curtain goes on the inside of the bathtub."' Perhaps you can understand why he might say that. So much damage in motel rooms is caused by people not remembering that. It may sound utterly ludicrous to us, but that is an important matter to him.

This is what is central to Yahweh: not tithes, not sacrifices, not building programmes, but *other gods*. That is what the problem is: the first commandment — Exodus 20:3: 'You shall have no other gods besides me.'

Now pagan people at that time, whether they were nice or nasty pagans, would find this bizarre: that Yahweh should insist on no other gods. They just could not comprehend it. It is like the situation I read about in a line-up at a police station. There was one thug there who had been caught raiding a delicatessen. He was a kind of beetle-browed, hard-looking fellow. He was questioned and searched. He had a few personal possessions, among them some brass knuckles. He somewhat sheepishly told the officer inspecting them, 'Take it easy with them knuckles, Sarge, they mean something to me.' Sure enough, on the inside of the little finger there was an inscription: 'With truest love, from Mildred.'

You probably find that strange because you do not ordinarily associate brass knuckles with romantic love, but people in the States do strange things. It does not seem to fit, does it? We just don't get it. And this did not fit in the ancient near east. Whoever heard of a god who demanded exclusive loyalty? There was no so-called god or goddess in the whole ancient near east who demanded exclusive devotion. Ishtar did not care if you worshipped Marduk part of the time. They did not care if you had a private shrine to some oak tree in your garden. It did not matter. It was OK. They were very tolerant. Why was this God utterly intolerant of any rivals?

It is because there was something in Israel called the covenant. That covenant was exclusive, like a marriage covenant, with Yahweh as the husband and Israel as his bride. It was to be an exclusive relationship. Any time, of course, that there is a breach in an exclusive relationship it ought to drive the one who is wronged into a fury. There is a proper kind of jealousy in love, and if it is not there, there is something wrong with the love. If the wife or the husband is being unfaithful, the other does not just say, 'Well, you win some, you lose some.' No, it should make you angry. It should infuriate you. It should stir up the proper jealousy of love. That is what you have in the fury of Yahweh, when he says, 'They have forsaken me; they have burned incense to other gods; they have bowed down to the works of their hands.' There ought to be a fire in love. And there is with Yahweh.

Of course, we are a little bit different from Judah. The problem with us is not some graven image as such. Our idols are a little more sophisticated. It might be fixation on our future. It might be security or comfort or addiction. It may be a little harder to detect. But Yahweh is simply fanatical in his Word about exclusive devotion to him.

You might say, 'Well then, what does he want?' We can put it positively. It was put positively very early on in Deuteronomy 6:4-5. It is Israel's creed: 'Hear, O Israel, Yahweh is our God; Yahweh alone. And you shall love Yahweh your God with your whole heart and your whole being and with everything you have.'

I am a little bit disturbed at some of the more recent Bible translations because they leave out the conjunction 'and' in Deuteronomy 6:5. I think probably English stylists decided, 'We don't want a lot of these "ands". We'll clean it up just a little bit. We'll start mostly new statements in Deuteronomy 6:5 etc.' So you have to go back to the original edition of the New American Standard Bible or the old RSV; the ESV or the NIV will not help you here. They drop the 'and'. But I like the literal grammar here because it is important theologically.

When he says the creed, 'Hear, O Israel, Yahweh is our God, Yahweh alone', that creed has glue on it, as all doctrine does. It has stickability. You do not make a confession of faith which does not carry any punch. Rather, when you say, 'Yahweh is our God and Yahweh alone', there is an 'and' that goes with it, a demand attached. If that is true, then that is what you must do: 'AND you shall love Yahweh your God with your whole heart, with your whole being and with everything you have.' That last phrase is 'with all your muchness', with everything you have. That is all Yahweh wants from you. No other god demanded that kind of devotion from his people.

You may be saying, 'Ah, yes, but Davis, you're holding us captive in the Old Testament. It's very bad, because if we can only get to the New Testament, we can get to Jesus. There will be mercy and grace. There won't be this pickiness. Back here we are still in the time of the law. I think I'll run into the New Testament and into the arms of Jesus and I won't have this problem.'

I can only say, 'Don't do it!' Such thinking reminds me of Wilmer McLean, who was a wholesale grocer for a while till he retired in about 1861. He was at a farm near a stream called Bull Run where the first major battle in the War Between the States took place. In his home a pot of stew was cooking on the fire and a shell from the Union army fell down the chimney and exploded in the stew! When McLean realized how his location would expose him to constant danger, he moved to a remote rural area in southern Virginia to escape all contact with the war. He settled in Appomattox Courthouse. But in 1865 this was the very place where Robert E. Lee's army surrendered to General Grant, and it was in his very parlour that the terms of peace were signed and sealed. His home was later ransacked for souvenirs. Wilmer tried to run away from the war, but the war caught up with him!

So if you try to get away from this fanatical God of the Old Testament, you will run straight into his arms in the New Testament when you go to Jesus. Remember what Jesus said in Matthew 10: 'Whoever loves father and mother more than me is not worthy of me, and whoever loves son or daughter more than me is not worthy of me. And whoever does not take his cross and follow me is not worthy of me.' We can translate that! It is an expanded version of 'You shall have no other gods before me.' Have you thought of that? How can Jesus of Nazareth stand there and with a straight face demand to have the supreme place of affection in your life? Who does he think he is? We cannot escape it. The Word of God is so astounding because it is so fanatical.

Conclusion

So what should God's astounding Word in Jeremiah do for you? It should comfort you in that it is relentless and fragile. It should instruct you in that it is so dominating and it should alarm you because it is so fanatical. If it does, it should bring you to repentance under the only shelter there ever is — the cross of Jesus.

2

Can this prophet be saved?

Jeremiah 15:10-21

You may not have an avid interest in prophets in general, but your curiosity might be aroused if you could peep into a prophet's memoirs or read part of his journal. I want to introduce you to part of Jeremiah's memoirs and bring you up to speed on the book. If you look at chapters 2 - 10 you see the content of Jeremiah's preaching; and nearly all of it is judgement, doom and gloom — that is the emphasis of his preaching. Then in chapters 11-20 there is another dominant theme, the prophet's conflicts. Alternatively, you could look at chapters 2 - 10 as the preaching of the Lord's judgement and chapters 11 - 20 as the problems of the Lord's servant. The problems are not wholly Jeremiah's, but the theme of the difficulties encountered by the Lord's servant occurs predominantly in chapters 11 - 20. The relentless preaching of judgement by Jeremiah was not appreciated. The hostility and the opposition that it generated against Jeremiah began to affect him and wear him down. In these periods, Jeremiah speaks to God in his discouragement. These pieces are sometimes referred to by scholars as Jeremiah's confessions, little clips of despair or discouragement where he pours out his soul to the Lord, and we have one of these confessions in chapter 15.

Jeremiah's complaint

Preface (15:10-14)

As we set the stage for Jeremiah's complaint, we shall consider verses 10-14 briefly. First of all, you find part of the complaint in verse 10, where Jeremiah is speaking: 'Woe to me, my mother, that you have given birth to me, a man of strife and a man of quarrelling for the whole land.' Then verse 11 begins with 'Yahweh said…', and so we have Yahweh's words all the way through to verse 14, containing his specific message to Jeremiah. Notice that the complaint is immediately followed by a word of assurance on Yahweh's part: 'Surely I will set you free for good. Surely I will make the enemy entreat with you…' (v. 11). That is the word of assurance to Jeremiah.

Then verse 12 is a re-emphasis of the truth of Jeremiah's message, as best as I can discern. The Lord still seems to be speaking. He says, 'Can one break iron, iron from the north, and bronze?' It seems to me that what the Lord is saying in that very succinct statement is that the message remains the same and is unalterable. The message of judgement cannot be changed. It is like iron, not like pipe cleaners that you can bend and twist any way you wish. This is like iron, iron from the north, and bronze. The message stands.

In verses 13-14 Yahweh seems to be speaking to the people of Judah — again, in summary, a re-emphasis and insistence on what is coming. 'Your wealth and your treasure I will give as plunder'; then in verse 14: 'I will make you serve your enemies in a land you do not know.' There is this re-emphasis on the coming captivity, probably of Judah going to Babylon.

That is the preface. I want now to take you through Jeremiah's experience as it is recorded especially in verses 15-21. It is not because you or I are prophets. I am not a prophet who receives direct divine revelation from God. I cannot say, 'As it was with Jeremiah, so it is with me.' It is a different situation. But there are aspects of Jeremiah's experience as a prophet here that overlap with the experience of any Christian disciple, and this is what I want to underscore.

Balancing on a paradox (15:15-17)

'You know, Yahweh. Remember me and care for me and take vengeance for me on my pursuers and do not — due to your longsuffering — take me away. It's for your sake that I have borne abuse. Your words were found and I ate them and your words became to me the joy and delight of my heart, for your name is called over me, O Yahweh, God of Hosts.'

You have two elements here. In verse 16, you have the joy of Yahweh's Word that Jeremiah celebrates: 'Your words were found and I ate them, and O what a joy and a delight they became to me.' God communicates his revelation. Jeremiah imbibes it fully and finds his highest pleasure as he assimilates God's Word. It is such a delight, because it is God's Word. It reveals God himself, even if it is a severe Word. It still reflects the character and the ways and the plan of God, and that always delights the servant of God. So there is the joy of Yahweh's Word in verse 16.

Now notice how that is wrapped around in verses 15 and 17 with the costliness of Yahweh's call. What is the costliness of his call? Well, you see opposition in verse 15, and you see it in two forms. He says, 'Take vengeance for me on my pursuers.' He is in danger — that kind of opposition. Then you notice at the end of verse 15, he is suffering abuse and ridicule: 'It's for your sake that I have borne abuse.' You have those two forms of opposition.

You get a picture of the first in his pursuers in chapter 11:18-23 and also in chapter 18:18-23. In 11:18-23 the Lord tells Jeremiah that even the men of Anathoth, his home town, are plotting against him. They say to him something like, 'You'd better stop this sort of preaching, because if you keep speaking in the name of the Lord this way, we are going to silence you and you'll never speak again.' It is a threat against his life. He is in physical danger if he goes on prophesying and speaking the Lord's Word. That is what he faced — a threat to his life from his own people in his home town.

Then there is the abuse at the end of verse 15. You have examples of that in 5:12-13, where there seemed to be people in Judah mocking the very idea of judgement that Jeremiah was proclaiming. They said, 'No disaster is going to come upon us. The prophets who speak that way are windbags. Do you see any disaster? Has judgement come? No!' It was that kind of attitude.

The same sort of thing is reflected in chapter 20:7-8. Jeremiah was upset because he had to proclaim violence and destruction and they apparently ridiculed him because it had not happened. 'Maybe you're a false prophet, Jeremiah.' In Jeremiah 20 a fellow called Pashhur placed Jeremiah in the stocks overnight; and when he let him out in the morning, Jeremiah (and it was a courageous move) said, 'Your name is not Pashhur but Magor-missabib [Terror on every side].' Then he told Pashhur what he was going to face when Babylon came into the land. But later in chapter 20, in verse 10, the people apparently threw this back in Jeremiah's face. They started repeating: 'Terror on every side!' Whenever Jeremiah appeared, they said, 'Look there. There's Terror on every side.' That is the opposition — constant ridicule and abuse.

In verse 17 we note that the costliness also involves isolation. Jeremiah says, 'I have not sat in the circle of those who party; nor did I celebrate. Because of your hand I sat alone, for you have filled me with indignation.' That isolation in verse 17 is fleshed out in chapter 16. Jeremiah is to be unique as a Hebrew man. He is not to get married. The Lord tells him in chapter 16 that he is not to have sons or daughters, because they would be doomed to die; they would face pestilence and famine, so he must not get married. He did not have what I sometimes call the built-in anti-depressant that some of us enjoy. Some of you who may have pastors who are single need to be aware of that. I do not mean that you have to hover over them and smother them, but just remember — they do not have the natural companionship and support that some of us married pastors have. That solitariness can play on you. Jeremiah is not to have a wife; he is not to have children (16:1-4). In addition, the Lord says 'No going to funerals. If you go to funerals, you might be tempted to try to comfort somebody.' And the Lord says, 'there is no comfort for this people; so don't go to funerals' (*cf.* 16:5-7). Then he says, 'Do not go to parties or weddings either. I've taken my peace away from this land.' So, no weddings, no parties, no celebrations (*cf.* 16:8-9). Utter isolation, terrible loneliness.

So there is opposition and isolation. But there is still another part to this costliness — a certain restriction. It is not here in this section of chapter 15; but if you go back you will notice other passages like 11:14; 14:11-12; 15:1. You might think that if Jeremiah suffers such opposition, if he is so isolated and alone, at least he can pray for these people, at least he can give himself up to a ministry of intercession. But the Lord says, 'No. Don't do that. It's not your fault, Jeremiah. Even if it were Moses and Samuel that were interceding with me I would not listen to them. The people are beyond prayer. It's too late for that' (15:1). There is an unchangeable doom that these people are under. So intercession is '*verboten*'. That is what he faced.

So do you see the paradox? You have the joy of Yahweh's Word (v. 16) and you have the costliness of Yahweh's call (vv. 15 and 17), and both are there together. You are balancing on a paradox.

There are similar examples in life. I am not a music historian, but Patrick Kavanaugh has a short description of Franz Joseph Haydn, the Austrian composer. Haydn had a very buoyant temperament. He was cheerful, finding joy and delight in his music and composing. In fact, Haydn said, 'Since God has given me a cheerful heart he will forgive me for serving him cheerfully.' It is a delightful little twist, isn't it? But Haydn had a different situation in his own home. As a young man he fell in love and was stunned when the girl ran off to a convent. So, impulsively, he proposed to her older sister and she, unfortunately, accepted the proposal! They were utterly incompatible. This new bride of Haydn's had so little regard for his composing genius that Patrick Kavanaugh says she cut up his manuscripts to use for hair-curler papers. Do you see the paradox, the two sides of that? Here is a man with this delightful, buoyant spirit and cheerful disposition; and on the other hand he is married to a battleaxe! You have those two things combined, that paradox. How do you pull that together? That is what you have with Jeremiah and that is what you have in the normal Christian life, don't you?

You remember what Paul says in Philippians 3 in that marvellous verse, 'That I may know him and the power of his resurrection' (v. 10). What does that involve? To know Jesus is to know transformation of character, liberation from bondage, power through distress and difficulties; it is to know the power of his resurrection.

Some people today think that this is all that knowing Jesus involves, that it is just the hoopla of the power and the glory. But there is an 'and' in that sentence. What does knowing Jesus mean? 'To know the power of his resurrection AND the fellowship of his sufferings, being shaped like him in his death.' Paul is saying that if you are going to know Jesus, you are going to be balancing on a paradox. There is going to be a 'both/and': there is going to be a certain tension in God's truth. So does God grant mighty deliverances and amazing providences and solid pleasures to those who serve him?

Can this prophet be saved?

Yes, but faith does not guarantee immunity from terrible distress and need. If Jeremiah gives us any clue it is that in his mysterious mercy and in his strange kindness God may not bring us out of our miseries in our lifetime. It is balancing on a paradox of delight and distress.

Stepping over a line (15:18)

Let me indicate briefly the position I think we need to take on verse 18. I refer to 18a for the first half of the verse and 18b for the second. Basically, I think it goes like this: 18a is permissible but 18b is not.

Perhaps, especially if you are a pastor, you have met people who at the end of a worship service shake your hand and make a comment like: 'Well, I know we're not supposed to ask why.' Such comments always distress me. You do not hear Scripture saying, 'We're not supposed to ask why.' You may not get an answer. You may not resolve the mystery. But Scripture encourages you to ask those questions. So you can anguish over God's timing: 'How much longer, Yahweh, will you forget me — for ever?' (Ps. 13). You can question God's ways and seeming inattention: 'Why, O Yahweh, do you stand far away? Why do you hide yourself in times of trouble?' (Ps. 10). You can express the futility of prayer: 'Every day I call upon you, Yahweh; I spread out my hands to you' (Ps. 88:9). The implication in that psalm is that prayer does not change things. It does not seem to change anything, but I am still praying. You can bemoan God's absence: 'My God, my God, why have you forsaken me? Why are you so far from saving me and from the words of my groaning?' (Ps. 22). You see the freedom that we have with our God. He does not say, 'You're not supposed to ask why', or any nonsense like that. But you can go too far, as Jeremiah did at the end of verse 18. I do not think the text reads as a question here, but rather a statement: 'You really are like a deceitful brook to me.'

The image of a deceitful brook is probably a reference to the seasonal streams, the wadis, in Israel. They might fill up in the rainy season and there might be plenty of water there, but in the dry season they are as dry as a bone. You may be there at a transitional time, hoping to find some water, but there is none, and that may be the idea behind the image: 'You really are to me as a deceitful brook.'

Now most of the English translations probably translate this as a question. They continue the question of the previous first half of the verse. That may be legitimate; but the construction in the Hebrew text is one that is more likely to be an emphatic statement. 'You really are to me like a deceitful brook, like waters that are not dependable.' That is really an accusation. Jeremiah is assaulting Yahweh's character; Jeremiah has stepped over a line.

I think we need to understand that this is possible. I think we need to understand in the psycho-slanted age in which we live, with its 'Let it all hang out' attitude, that you can step over the line in your complaining to God. In a previous age we may have been overly cautioned about this; in our day we may not be cautioned enough.

H. L. Ellison highlighted the danger this way. He wrote, 'There is a widespread belief in certain circles that anything that comes welling up from the depths of my being with almost irresistible force must be from the Holy Spirit.' In other words, if you question people like that they might say, 'But this is how I really feel.' Sometimes when you really feel that way, the best response is to keep quiet. In other words, anguish must not dissolve reverence, especially when you realize that it is still this God alone who gives you the very breath that you use to express your despair.

So bemoan his mysteries. You have that freedom. Bemoan his mysteries, but do not assault his majesty. Do not deny his character. Do not step over that line.

Can this prophet be saved?

Coming under an ultimatum (15:19)

Jeremiah records Yahweh's response: 'Therefore, if you return I will restore you. You can stand before me and if you bring forth what is precious rather than what is worthless, you can be as my mouth. They may turn to you, but you must not turn to them.'

Now what is going on here? This may not be the response we expect from the Lord; but here is Yahweh's reply, and it turns on a verb that is used four times in the text. The English translation probably has to use different words; it is hard to use the same one in each case. But it is the verb 'to return' or 'to turn'. That is the basic idea. It is a common verb that is used of repenting of sin or error. But you see, when Yahweh says in the first part of the verse, 'If you return I will cause you to return,' we have to render that something like 'If you return I will restore you.' But it is the same verb. Then in the last part of the verse he says, 'They [that is, the people] may turn [the same verb again] to you but you, Jeremiah, you must not turn to them.' It all revolves around this verb that is repeated four times.

What he is saying is that Jeremiah can come back. He can be reinstated, as it were, in his office as prophet. 'If you return, if you repent, I will restore you. You can go on prophesying again. You can be as my mouth. You can stand before me and function as a prophet and speak my Word. But it all depends on your response, Jeremiah.'

Then you notice how those last two uses of 'turn' or 'return' at the end of verse 19 chart Jeremiah's duty. 'They may turn to you, but you must not turn to them. They may turn toward your message, they may accept that. If they are willing to, that's all right, they may turn to you. They can accept your message if they will, but you must not turn to them. You must not cave in and preach a positive message to them that I have not given you; you may want to, you may long to preach a comforting word; you may long to hearten them. Every pore of your soul may want to preach a comforting word to them. You long to hear their response of appreciation. But you must not do it. You must not turn to them.' So that is what verse 19 seems to be emphasizing. The Lord is putting Jeremiah under an ultimatum.

So Jeremiah pours out his despair and then Yahweh says, 'Repent of your unbelief if you want to be restored.' Sometimes the Lord deals directly like that. A. W. Tozer tells of a time in his pastorate in Toronto, probably in the very late 1950s or 1960s. He said that not long after he arrived in Toronto a cultured, attractive young woman made an appointment to see him. She said she was troubled about a homosexual relationship with her room-mate. She had already talked with other professionals about this and Tozer had the distinct impression that she hoped that he would assure her that what she was doing was permissible in this day and age. Instead, he faced her squarely and said, 'Young woman, you are guilty of sodomy and God is not going to give you any approval or comfort until you turn from your known sin and seek his forgiveness and cleansing.' What was her response? 'I guess I needed to hear that,' she admitted.

Sometimes it is the direct retort that brings us up short. That is not always the way that the Lord deals with us, but it is one way that he may use and you see that here. He does not cuddle Jeremiah but rebukes him. He calls him to account and tells him to repent.

Now I want you to ponder that, because I think there is a sentiment abroad in Christian circles which says that Jesus would never do anything like that. Folks would, I suppose, rather rewrite John 21, which details that episode after Jesus' resurrection when he meets with the eleven disciples and especially confronts Peter. The first three Gospels have the Lord's Supper, but John has an account of the Lord's breakfast. (Sometime you may want to preach the Lord's breakfast passage when you have the Lord's Supper — it is very appropriate.)

But there is Jesus having a one-to-one with Peter. You remember what the text says, as Jesus stared across that fire with the fish on it and looked Peter in the eye. 'I don't want you to get down on yourself, Peter. Almost everyone messes up now and again. And you're a great person and you have a fabulous potential for ministry. I don't want to see your self-esteem go out the window. I want you to feel good about yourself.'

No, that is not in the text. Instead, he says, 'Simon, son of John, do you love me more than these?' He pressed him three times and Peter was grieved, he was hurt, and Jesus wanted him to be hurt, I think. He was pressing him. You see, you do not always meet the therapeutic Jesus; you do not always meet the psychological Jesus who coos to you: 'I understand how you must feel that way.' I am not undercutting what Hebrews 2 and 4 say about our great High Priest. But you do not always meet a Jesus made in your own mould. Sometimes you meet the one who says to you, 'Repent of your unbelief; repent of your coldness; repent of that chip on your shoulder; repent of your rebellion — and I will restore you.'

We are balancing on a paradox, we are stepping over a line, and we are coming under an ultimatum. Fourthly, we are resting in fresh assurance.

Resting in fresh assurance (15:20-21)

Now, typically, Yahweh does not merely rebuke. Even when he rebukes, there is often a word of encouragement; and you see that here.

Let us look at the text here in verse 20. Yahweh goes on to say: 'And I shall make you to this people a fortified bronze wall, and they shall fight against you but they will not get the best of you, for I am with you to save you and to deliver you, declares Yahweh, and I shall deliver you from the hand of evil men and I shall ransom you from the grip of ruthless men.' There is that assurance.

Part of this encouragement has been heard before. If you go back to Jeremiah 1:18-19 (the chapter in which Jeremiah was called), you meet this fortified bronze wall imagery. It is repeated here with some variation but obviously the same assurance.

So the important thing is that Yahweh is not telling Jeremiah anything new. He does not have a new secret for the Christian life or for prophetic ministry to give him. No! He simply brings home to him what he had already said. This fresh assurance is the old assurance stated once more in a new situation. I think that is important. He does not receive a new word; he receives an old word freshly applied in the current circumstance. That is an important fact because that is the way Scripture operates in the life of a servant of Christ as well.

Irene Howat has written a little book, *Finding God is in the darkness*, and in that book she tells of Pat Cardy. She and her husband were living in Northern Ireland around 1980 and their nine-year-old daughter Jennifer went to play with one of her friends. She started riding her bike over to her friend's house and they never saw her again. They found her body about a week later. She had been murdered. They did not know why, they did not know who. You can imagine the parents facing that situation. Pat Cardy relates how she was given grace to make it through Jennifer's funeral. But then she talks about the following day when she did not find any of that grace. She tried to busy herself tidying up and cleaning, but it did not work. She tried not to give in to tears as she saw and touched

Jennifer's belongings. Finally, she was in the bathroom and there again were Jennifer's own personal items, and the awful finality of death hit her. She said that once the tears started there was no holding back, and the violent, suffocating sobs kept coming. 'I would never see her again. I wished that I, too, could die.'

She began as best she could to call on God for help and for sustaining grace in that time. There followed another stream of bitter tears as she picked up her copy of *Daily Light* which was there in the bathroom. She said, 'I could read nothing. My tears were unwipable as well as unstoppable. Twice I tried to read … but I could not. The third time I read these words more clearly, "And God shall wipe away all tears from their eyes; and there shall be no more death, neither sorrow nor crying … for the former things are passed away" (Revelation 21:4, AV).' The whole page was full of Scriptures relating to that theme. And she said, 'I was conscious of the presence of the Lord Jesus, so intimate, so near, as one who wept with me.' What was that? Was that something new? No, it was an old word zeroed in on a new need.

In Iain Murray's biography of Martyn Lloyd-Jones he refers to some troubles Lloyd-Jones had in the summer of 1949. He went for recuperation, and where would he go but to Wales! He was apparently exhausted physically and was somewhat depressed. There were some difficulties and apparently a certain fear about his ability to keep going. All these things were pressing on him — it was a very difficult summer. He finally returned to London in September 1949. He was to preach at Westminster Chapel the next Sunday 11 September. He had been thinking about his sermon, but he reached Saturday afternoon and nothing had come. It was as if the fountain had dried up, as if there was nothing there and he could not preach, and all his concerns were coming back. Lloyd-Jones said he was in his study that afternoon in a kind of near despair, and 'there came into my mind from Titus 1:2 that phrase,

"God who cannot lie"'. You remember: 'Eternal life, which God, who cannot lie, promised us long ages ago.' And he said he was utterly overwhelmed, he was in tears, and the sermon was given to him there and then.

You say, what difference can that text make? Well, just the fact that it highlights the very character of your God; and if you are in the pit, what do you need? You need the assurance that you have a God who always speaks the truth to you, who is utterly reliable. Does that take away the pit? No, the sides may still be slimy and it may be horrible in there. But if you know that it is not a bottomless pit, if you know that the faithfulness of God has built a floor in the pit, you know you cannot go down any further than that. 'God who cannot lie' — that captures you when you slide. But again, you see, it was not some new truth. It was the old truth and the same God, freshly revealed.

In 1854 Charles Spurgeon had been ministering for about a year in London. In the neighbourhood where he served, the Asiatic cholera hit and his congregation suffered from the inroads of that. He said that family after family summoned him to the bedside of someone or other. He would be called to visit the graveside almost every day; and at first, in his youth and enthusiasm, he gave himself up to this ministry with real gusto. But then as he was sent for by people of all types to minister to them and as he had to bury friends and ones he had come to love, it began to wear him down and he was weary in body and sick at heart. He thought he himself was becoming sick as well.

He said, 'I was ready to sink down under it; and one day as I was walking back from a funeral, as God would have it my curiosity led me to read a paper that was pasted on a shoemaker's window on the Great Dover Road. It was a huge piece of paper and on it in good, bold handwriting were these words: "Because thou hast made the Lord thy refuge, even the Most High thy habitation, there shall no evil befall thee, neither shall any plague come nigh thy dwelling."' He said, 'The effect upon my heart was immediate. Faith appropriated the passage as her own. I felt secure, refreshed, girt with immortality. I went on with the visitation of the dying in a calm, peaceful spirit. I felt no fear of evil and I suffered no harm.'

Now what was that? Well, blessed be shoemakers who plaster up Psalm 91:9-10 in their shop windows. But it was not some new truth, was it? It was not a 'word of knowledge' someone jazzed up out of the blue. No, this was old truth that had already been given and it was freshly applied to a new situation. That is the way Jesus works, but we can forget this; we can forget that Jesus in his offices or functions is prophet, priest and king. And Jesus in his office as prophet is the one who speaks the Word of God to us. Isaiah 50:4 describes him as the servant of Yahweh, who knows how to sustain the weary with a word. He does it by applying the Scriptures to our needs.

We value Christian booksellers and publishers who give us such excellent material; but we do not need a new book on every new problem we face, when we have the Word that Christ freshly applies to our souls. We have old assurances in new circumstances.

Now stand back from Jeremiah 15 and get a little perspective on it. Just think about it and think about what a marvellous miracle it is that folks like Jeremiah, and other servants of Christ like him, can get the stuffing knocked out of them and yet they will say, 'I will still serve him.' Peter is right. 'Lord, to whom shall we go? You have the words of eternal life.'

3

The yoke is no joke

Jeremiah 27 - 29

Several months ago in the United States we had a Toyota scare over safety matters. One was about an accelerator that sometimes would accelerate when it was not supposed to accelerate! Now imagine a group of Toyota executives at a meeting and you go in wearing a Toyota accelerator pedal on a chain around your neck. That would cause some embarrassment, to say the least. We do not like bad news, and we do not like to be reminded of bad news.

What if you heard that your nation would be overrun, decimated and dominated by the new superpower; that everyone who told you otherwise was lying; that the majority of the population would be transported to live in the land of the conquerors; that this situation would go on for some years with no possibility of change; and that this was because God had decided that it would be so? That was the way it was with Judah in Jeremiah's day.

If you were one of those who were still clinging to Yahweh and seeking to walk before him in righteousness in the midst of a mostly apostate nation and facing this imminent judgement, you were called to live under that plan of God in such nasty times.

It seems to me that we can sum up the testimony of Jeremiah 27 - 29 in this way — God sometimes decrees a course of history which his people cannot welcome enthusiastically but in which they must live faithfully.

Principle: There is a decree that controls politics
(chapter 27)

King Zedekiah (this is not in the text but we can imagine the situation) suddenly flushed crimson. He was coming out of the building into the courtyard where conference folks were gathering and he saw Jeremiah! He was so embarrassed that he retreated into the men's room to try to gather his thoughts, because the prophet Jeremiah was plodding into the teatime break of the East Mediterranean summit in Jerusalem and he was wearing an ox's yoke around his neck. No Toyota accelerator pedal for him, but an ox's yoke! He was bending the ear of the diplomat from Moab and he was saying to him, 'This is what I want to tell you. This is what Yahweh says.' He was making the rounds of the folks from Ammon and Tyre and Sidon and giving them the same message.

What was his message to these envoys? Probably they were only there stirring up trouble and trying to confer as to whether they should submit to or throw off the control and dominance of Babylon, but Jeremiah was telling these men that in fact Yahweh, the God of Israel, was sovereign and that he was imposing his sovereign plan on them, and that his plan meant that their countries would be subservient to Nebuchadnezzar and Babylon.

The text underscores the sovereignty, the kingship, the total dominance of Yahweh over history. We need to look at what Jeremiah tells us of God's sovereignty, because it is that sovereignty which decrees the way history goes.

The yoke is no joke

A surprising sovereignty

You see a surprising sovereignty in what Jeremiah tells these conference delegates. You notice in verse 4 that he is to give them this charge for their masters: 'Thus says Yahweh of hosts, the God of Israel...' Well, that is interesting. The NIV has 'the LORD Almighty', but the more traditional rendering is 'Yahweh of hosts'. What kind of hosts? Sometimes the term refers to an angelic host (*cf.* 1 Kings 22:19; Ps. 103:20-21), to a celestial host (Deut. 4:19), or to earthly armies (e.g. Israel's, Ps. 44:9). The point is that all the resources and all the powers in the universe, seen and unseen, are under Yahweh's control and at his disposal — he is Yahweh of hosts, the God of Israel.

The whole expression is a strange mix! It is like saying, 'Yahweh of hosts, the God of Vermont'; or, 'Yahweh of hosts, the God of Yorkshire'. If the Lord is really supreme over everything, he could do better than be called, for example, 'the God of Israel'. If he is really that great a God, why would he be the God of a little postage-stamp-sized kingdom called Judah? That is a conundrum. It is a surprising sovereignty. But it is vital to understand that appearances are not necessarily the guide to truth.

I attended a small church college in Kansas, and one professor used to tell a story about a period earlier in the college's existence. I am not sure if they were working on some college buildings or what, but a group of men were busy working and one man was moving some materials to the worksite in a wheelbarrow. He was a real dumpy-looking fellow who did not even have a belt — his trousers were held up by a piece of rope tied through the front belt loops. In fact, he was Dr Calhoun, the academic dean of the college! He had grey matter coming out of his ears! You cannot tell from impressions.

So Yahweh does not need a marketing boost from us. He is not the little God of Israel; he is the God of little Israel. There is a big difference. So his kingship and his worldwide sway do not depend on how impressive his people are. It is a surprising sovereignty in the way it is expressed.

A proper sovereignty

It is a proper sovereignty. Consider verse 5, where Yahweh says, 'It is I who by my great power and my outstretched arm have made the earth, with the men and animals that are on the earth, and I give it to whomever it seems right to me' (ESV). He gives it because it is his and he can do what he pleases with what belongs to him. 'The earth is Yahweh's and the fulness thereof, the world and those who dwell therein, for he has founded it upon the seas and established it upon the rivers' (Ps. 24:1-2). It is his to give. He can do what he wants with it.

The words in the text could be considered almost a parallel to Jesus' parable in Matthew 20:15 about the vineyard owner. 'Am I not allowed to do what I choose with what belongs to me?' That is sovereignty, and that is what Yahweh is saying here. This is a proper sovereignty. 'I can dispose of my world in the way that I choose to because it is mine.' There is a freedom there.

A particular sovereignty

It is also a particular sovereignty. This sovereignty is not some vague, theoretical idea; rather, Yahweh speaks of his supremacy in terms of names and dates. Look at verses 6-7: 'Now I have given all these lands into the hand of Nebuchadnezzar, the king of Babylon, my servant, and I have given him also the beasts of the field to serve him. All the nations shall serve him and his son and his grandson, until the time of his own land comes' (ESV). There is a definite, particular element in that sovereignty. We do not always see it, because he does not disclose details to us; but here he does name names and fill in blanks.

The yoke is no joke

In the War Between the States in my country, Jefferson Davis was the president of the Confederate States for about four years. He had jurisdiction over all sorts of things, running a war and all the matters of government. But there were all sorts of things that came across his desk, and in one instance a request came from a young lady in South Carolina who was concerned that she could not get her beau home from the army so that they could get married. So she had written to Jefferson Davis. The soldier's name was Jeems and she, as one writer says, had more heart than grammar. In her letter to President Davis she said that she wanted her fiancé to come home from the army in order to marry her. She wrote this way: 'Jeems is willing; I is willing; his mammy says she is willing; but Jeems' captain, he ain't willing. Now when we are willing, 'cepting Jeems' captain, I think you might let up and let Jeems come.' She even promised to make her beloved return to the army as soon as they had exchanged their vows. President Davis turned the paper over and, before he sent it on to the Secretary of War, wrote on the back, 'Let Jeems go.'

You mean that President Davis would stoop to matters like that? Yes, he was in control of all sorts of things and he had jurisdiction over all sorts of matters, even down to grubby details if he liked — and in that case he did. It had to do with an ungrammatical girl from South Carolina who wanted to get married and he authorized it.

And in Jeremiah, the way Yahweh runs his world is by giving it into the hand of this cocky, swaggering Nebuchadnezzar whom he calls 'my servant', and this arrangement is going to continue for some time. These nations are going to serve Nebuchadnezzar and his son and his grandson until the time of his own land comes. It is a particular sovereignty, and Jeremiah was telling these conference delegates that this was a decree from the God who runs history and that they were not to listen to the false prophets and diviners who were telling them otherwise.

Jeremiah was pressing this message on these near eastern delegates. There is a decree that controls politics, and this is how it is being controlled right now, and they all need to submit to Yahweh's programme. That was the point.

But it seems to me that there is something else about this sovereignty here that perhaps points to how we should respond to this ancient word about politics that Jeremiah has spoken — we can call it a sobering sovereignty.

A sobering sovereignty

There is a clause in verse 7 that haunts me: 'All the nations shall serve him and his son and his grandson, until the time of his own land comes...' It appears that Yahweh is supporting the superpower of the day. But that sovereignty can pack a message for all superpowers — 'until the time of their own land comes'.

When I made this point in my own congregation, I had to say that this applies to contemporary so-called superpowers as well. Sometimes the USA is called a superpower. But in spite of all the privileges of our country, in spite of all the godly intentions of some of the early settlers, in spite of the relative degree of justice that has been enjoyed in our land over a number of years — and you have to say this because in our situation there are even some professing Christians who have a hard time drawing the line between patriotism and faith — nevertheless, the United States is not the covenant people of God. You have to say that our nation is not the chosen race. We do not have manifest destiny. We are on the whole a pagan people; we are an immoral people, a covetous people, an ungrateful people, a wicked nation, and we are ripe for the judgement of God. There will be a time in his sovereignty when the time of our own land comes. It is a sobering sovereignty.

This is so for people in the UK as well. In the various countries that make up this nation you have had vast privileges over the years. Just thinking of the last several hundred years, you have been a conduit of light, the light of the gospel, to many places on earth. The blazes of revival have touched down in many places, not only cities but hamlets all over your countries. What privileges!

But even you have to face that you are in the hand of this sovereign God who has decreed and determined politics and directs history. Surely you have to say, 'Oh, yes, there may be a time when the time of our own land comes.' That is the principle: there is a decree that controls politics.

Now we meet with a problem, namely, that there is a dilemma that involves truth in chapter 28.

Problem: There is a dilemma that involves truth
(chapter 28)

We know what Jeremiah said in chapter 27, but what if someone else tells you something different? What if someone else apparently has a different word from the Lord? Well, that happened in a very public venue. Hananiah proclaimed in Jeremiah 28:2-4 the very opposite of what Jeremiah had said. Hananiah said, 'Thus says Yahweh of hosts, the God of Israel: I have broken the yoke of the king of Babylon. Within two years I will bring back to this place all the vessels of Yahweh's house, which Nebuchadnezzar king of Babylon took away from this place and carried to Babylon' (ESV alt.).

Notice that Hananiah did not say 'I think' or 'perhaps'. He did not say, 'Jeremiah, I beg to differ.' He said, 'Thus says Yahweh of hosts';

the same formula, the same certainty, the same note of authority — he even picked up the symbolism in verses 10-11 and reversed it. He took that yoke that was on Jeremiah's neck and broke it. It is like a faith healer who takes away somebody's crutches and heaves them off the stage. All the people probably clapped; it was great stuff. Church was so much fun when Hananiah was there!

And it was a positive message. It came with certainty and vigour, with impressiveness and stage effects. Who to believe? Who has the truth? There is a problem, a dilemma that involves truth. How do you know the truth of the matter?

In World War II, the Germans would frequently modify or replace their radar and communications equipment; and almost as soon as they did, the British would manufacture new jamming devices. There was an airborne jammer that could be installed in British planes to jam some of the German signals so that the Germans had to resort to some very high-powered transmitters to give radio and telephone instructions to their night fighters.

Then the RAF set up a high-powered station to broadcast on the same frequency and certain ghost voices began echoing the German ground controllers. Sometimes they would broadcast contrary instructions and misleading information to the German night fighter pilots. The ghosts, the British voices that were on the frequency, spoke idiomatic German and even trained themselves to mimic the inflections of the German ground controllers.

In October 1943 in an RAF raid on a German city, the Germans realized that something was wrong. The RAF monitors were apparently at work. One German controller told his night fighter pilots to beware of another voice and warned them not to be led astray by the enemy. After a particularly violent outburst by one German controller, one of the ghost voices said, 'The Englishman is swearing!' — which brought a response from the German saying, 'It's not the Englishman who is swearing but me!' For German pilots it could be sheer mayhem.

Well, that is the problem. Whom do you believe and to whom do you listen? Jeremiah has one message and Hananiah has another, and they both seem equally certain and dogmatic. When I was very young I would sometimes pick up the British Israelite Worldwide Church of God on the radio and hear Garner Ted Armstrong. He could speak so forcefully that it sounded like the truth. It had that authoritative tone to it. How do you know what to do with such claims and such 'authority'?

Well, with Jeremiah in chapter 28, you notice a couple of matters. Jeremiah made what you might call an interim comment in verses 6-9, basically saying something like this: 'Hananiah, I hope that what you have prophesied will come true.' He does not say when that may be. 'But you are going against the prophetic tradition, which seems to prophesy times of war and judgement and famine and pestilences.' Then he continues in verse 9: 'for the prophet who has an optimistic message and prophesies peace and welfare as you have done, when the word of that prophet comes to pass, then we know that Yahweh has truly sent the prophet. And in the meantime we suspend judgement.' That is one possibility. We wait for the fulfilment.

Then the Lord communicated a further word to Jeremiah in verses 12-14 to update him, and basically he said, 'Hananiah may have broken that wooden yoke, but I am imposing an iron yoke, bars of iron, and these nations will serve Nebuchadnezzar king of Babylon. It is a sure thing.'

Then in verses 15-17 Jeremiah did something apparently at the direction of the Lord. He said to Hananiah, 'Yahweh has not sent you. You have made this people trust in a lie. Therefore, here is what Yahweh says: "I will remove you from the face of the earth. This year you shall die because you have uttered rebellion against Yahweh"' (vv. 15b-16a). In that same year, in the seventh month, the prophet Hananiah died. That was apparently, according to Jeremiah 28:1, two months after the altercation between Hananiah and Jeremiah. That ought to have been an indication and a preview of where the truth stood, because when the folks in Jerusalem read Hananiah's obituary in the *Jerusalem Post* a few days or weeks later, they should have said, 'Hmmm. He's the guy that prophesied and he has died. Jeremiah prophesied that he would die this year, and he has, within two months. That seems to indicate that if anyone has the word of the Lord it must be Jeremiah.' So that is the trick, detecting what is falsehood and what is truth.

A man went into a pharmacy in Yonkers, New York, a few years ago and handed a prescription to the pharmacist, who became suspicious and told him to come back in the afternoon. In the meantime he called the doctor and found out that this fellow had been to the doctor's, asking for a narcotic which the doctor had refused. So the fellow had stolen a prescription pad, gone home, looked the desired drug up in a book and very carefully transcribed the prescription. Why did the pharmacist get suspicious? The prescription was too legible to be written by a doctor! You have to have ways to know where the truth is.

How do you know? It is a problem. That is the set-up in 590 BC in our text, but do we not have the same problem today? Surely this is a continuing matter in our culture and among our churches. It is such an important matter.

In January 1987 in Oklahoma Oral Roberts launched a campaign. He told his followers that if he did not raise a total of $8 million by March of that year God was going to take his life. He said,

'God clearly told me he needs me here on earth because of all the ministries; this ministry is the only one God has on this earth that owns a medical school.' A little while later, his son Richard wrote: 'Without the additional $4,500,000 God will not extend Dad's life. God has shown me that this is going to happen.' How do you deal with that?

Well, you might say that you have the spiritual gift of cynical scepticism and that is how you deal with it. You say, 'I don't think Oral will become mute because of that. I don't think that will happen.' But the question is about truth. How do you determine the truth? This matter faces us again and again. You might not think it is so desperate and so necessary until it gets closer to home.

I remember about 1993 a member of our congregation was in my study, weeping. He was concerned over the spiritual state of his children. He did not think they were ready to meet the Lord and he was driven to tears. It was a tragic, sad thing — not because he was concerned about the spiritual status and position of his children, but because of why he had been driven to that state. A fairly well-respected radio preacher called Harold Camping had written a book called *1994*, and by some sort of harum scarum hermeneutics he was saying, 'Jesus is coming again in 1994.'

To read in 1993 that Jesus is coming again in 1994, bringing in the end of the world, causes this man in our congregation to be sitting in my study, weeping because it is happening next year and his kids are not ready! Applause for his concern, but the reason behind it is that he believed a false scriptural interpretation. It can make quite a difference. That is a problem.

All I can do is say to you in the words of Isaiah, 'To the teaching and to the testimony!' (Isa. 8:20) — and to you men especially, who are given the task of interpreting the Word of God to the people of God in the churches of Christ: be very careful that you stick closely to the claims of the Scriptures and do not go beyond them. Sometimes the whole state of an individual depends on how reliable you are in communicating the truth of the Scripture.

Prescription: There is a direction that governs life
(chapter 29:1-14)

Now we come to the prescription. In chapter 29 you are taken back to a time just prior to what actually happened in chapters 27 and 28. There was something Jeremiah had done, probably in about 597 BC or shortly after. There were different waves of the exile when the people of Judah were taken to Babylon, and one of the key exile years was 597 BC. It was the time when a number of the upper class and some of the artisans and metal workers were taken; but the final wave was in 587 BC. So some time after the previous wave in 597 BC, some emissaries from Judah had to go to Babylon, and Jeremiah gave them a letter to be communicated to the exiles of 597 BC about what Yahweh had given him to say about their settlement and distant future. We can just look briefly at his directions to these exiles who were already in Babylon.

An ordinary focus

Notice that there is an ordinary focus about what he is communicating to them. In verses 5-6, he tells them to build houses and live in them, to plant gardens, to grow and eat the produce, to take wives and have sons and daughters, to take wives for their sons and give their daughters in marriage so that they may bear sons and daughters, to multiply there and not decrease. In other words, they were to engage in the normal activities of life, to get houses built, plant gardens, grow food, get married, have children and keep on going — the daily stuff of life.

The yoke is no joke

A civic duty

Then in verse 7 he says that there is also a civic duty: 'But seek the welfare of the city where I have sent you into exile, and pray to Yahweh on its behalf; for in its welfare you will find your welfare.' Pray for Babylon. But it is a wicked, pagan empire! Yes, it is. But you want to seek its welfare because that is where you are going to be for a while. So it will be for your welfare to pray to Yahweh for its welfare. Pray for the city where you are going. Intercede before God for it. That is a civic duty.

A future hope

Then you notice that there is a future hope in verses 10-11. Jeremiah begins: 'When seventy years are completed for Babylon'. Not two years, as Hananiah said. 'When seventy years are completed for Babylon, I will visit you, and will fulfil to you my promise and bring you back to this place. For I know the plans I have for you, declares Yahweh, plans for welfare and not for evil, to give you a future and a hope' (ESV alt.). He has a plan with a future and a hope — but it is a delayed one, not an immediate one.

An immediate challenge

Then you notice an immediate challenge that he puts before these '597 exiles' in verses 12-14. The ESV starts verse 12 with: 'Then you will call upon me and come and pray to me and I will hear you.' That seems to give the impression that the calling and praying occur when the seventy years are completed. But a literal translation of the Hebrew would be 'and'. The ESV is just interpreting. Sometimes that is OK, but the 'then' is not necessarily a temporal 'then'. 'And you shall call upon me and come and pray to me and I will hear you, and you shall seek me and find me when you will seek me with all your heart, and I shall be found by you, declares Yahweh, and I shall restore your fortunes.'

It is not necessarily calling on Yahweh near the end of the seventy years. It can be done now. It can be done in the present time. They can begin to call upon Yahweh; they can begin to seek him with all their heart and he promises that he will be found by them. They must wait till he gives them the freedom to return in his time, but they can begin calling on him now. They can make the right response even in their present distress. That is how Jeremiah directs them. It has to do with an ordinary focus, a civic duty, a future hope and an immediate challenge.

Now what does this have to do with us? It seems long ago and far away and we are not exiles in Babylon. But are there not comparable situations, not just for bodies of the Lord's people but for individual believers? Could we not say that there can sometimes be situations that we face that are the same in principle, though far removed in terms of particulars?

Are there not situations where you or others of the Lord's people are placed in non-ideal situations, as Judah is here? Perhaps sometimes it has been brought about by your own sin and rebellion, and you have since repented of it and fellowship with the Lord has been restored; but there are still consequences that hang over your life, that press down on you because of it. Guilt is forgiven, fellowship restored; but sometimes the consequences are not eliminated. It is a non-ideal situation and you cannot fix it. You have to live through it.

We must live faithfully within a life situation that we do not like but cannot change. There is no immediate solution to our set of circumstances, but there is a way to be faithful. That is the situation here. Jeremiah is spelling out for those already in Babylon a way to be faithful even in a 'down' situation.

Some of us may be effervescent optimists who assume that most problems can be fixed. But there are lots of the Lord's people who live in circumstances and in conditions (sometimes brought on by sin, sometimes not) that are not fixable and not enjoyable, and yet they are called to be faithful.

Let me just give you one example. In Faith Cook's book *The Sound of Trumpets* she tells of a woman from north-east Scotland named Christian Watt. I think this illustrates in one individual such a situation.

By the time Christian Watt was eight or ten years old she had to work in the homes of wealthy people. She got up at 5.00am to do so. Tragedy struck the home and family, and one year five of her brothers died within six months. When she was about twenty-five years old she became pregnant. Unfortunately it was by her intended in a moment of temptation. It was during that time, though, that Christian Watt was converted. She said that as she was waiting for her child to be born, 'I read nothing but the Bible, and to my own joy and astonishment I found the Lord Jesus as my own personal Saviour.'

By the time she was thirty-four she had seven children below nine years of age. She was gutting and curing herring in order to supplement the family's meagre income. Then there were three more births. Later, one son was lost at sea and another to tetanus, and her husband was lost in a storm.

So she was a widow with eight children in pretty desperate circumstances. She had a dog, Ranger, and when no one was looking, she would wrap her arms around Ranger's neck and weep uncontrollably. She was just plain bereft. She said, 'I had my trust in Christ, the Man of Sorrows.' But the stress was so much that a doctor ordered her to go to an Aberdeen mental hospital for complete rest.

She came back apparently rested and renewed. The stigma of being in a mental hospital was another thing. She was ostracized. She tried to sell fish, but no one wanted to buy fish from a mad woman. So she found a job splitting and gutting fish. But one of the other women said, 'I think it is very wrong that a woman out of the asylum should be working with knives', and so she lost her job.

She tried to emigrate to the United States and when the application papers came back, she had been refused because of her medical record. Her mind snapped. She went to the henhouse that had only half a dozen under-nourished hens in it, and she tried to burn it down. But she was forcibly stopped, certified insane, and the next day taken to the mental institution for good.

She received adequate food and rest at the hospital and recovered her stability; but she was never able to go home again. What do you do in such a case? She worked in the kitchen and the laundry and she endeared herself to the staff. She could meet with new patients who came in suffering from nervous exhaustion as she had, and she could try to console them, and she spoke to them of her faith in the One who was the 'Man of Sorrows and acquainted with grief'.

That was not what she wanted. Do you want to end up for the rest of your life in a mental institution? No, it was not her preference; but there was nothing she could do. Those were the circumstances; those were the bounds that she had been given. Did she enjoy that? Did she plan for that? No, no. But you can be faithful to Jesus when you work in an asylum and point others to him even as you wash pots and pans in the kitchen. That is what the Lord is calling many of us to do. God calls us to live faithfully within the box of circumstances we cannot change. You may be in your Babylon, but you can still be there as a servant of Yahweh. That is a direction that governs life.

The yoke is no joke

So the yoke is no joke, but the yoke may not be so bad. There is a sovereign God over all the nations, who speaks truth in his Word and charges you to be faithful in your exile.

4

Jerusalem burning

Jeremiah 37 - 39

Our title is 'Jerusalem burning' and we are looking at Jeremiah chapters 37 - 39. We will be considering various texts from this section as I try to tie one theme together.

When I was about five or six years old I had an outfit that I wore every Sunday for church. I did not mind the top, which was a knitted sweater-like shirt, but I did not like the trousers; they were of a brown material and seemed baggy. Well, I did not feel happy with those trousers. So I decided that I would offer a little resistance.

There are two ways of offering resistance: one can be overt and blatant, or one can be subtle, indirect and devious; and I resolved upon the latter option. I took those trousers early one Sunday morning, folded them up and hid them in my room in the attic and told my Mum, 'I can't find my trousers,' hoping that she would in her despair say, 'Well, OK, you can wear your jeans.' That would have been marvellous. But my technique was that sort of devious, indirect, subtle kind of resistance. Sometimes that is the way we resist; and that is the kind of resistance you see in Zedekiah, the last king of Judah.

It is highlighted in 37:1-2 as Zedekiah is re-introduced; verse 2 says, 'Neither he nor his servants nor the people of the land listened to the words of Yahweh that he spoke through Jeremiah the prophet' (ESV alt.). There it is — resistance to the word of Yahweh.

Now it was the same song in a previous regime, for back in chapter 36 you hear of Jehoiakim, who could be described as a crass secularist. He was the one who cut up and burned the copies of Jeremiah's scroll. That was his in-your-face response. But Zedekiah is far more subtle.

To catch up on where we are in the prophecy of Jeremiah: we find that, after the introduction, chapters 2 - 10 contain a sample of Jeremiah's preaching; then chapters 11 - 20 begin to highlight the anguish of the prophet; and chapters 21 - 29 depict the shadow of Babylon as Yahweh speaks of Nebuchadnezzar as his servant, who would come in and dominate Judah. Then, although chapters 30 - 33 constitute a section of hope and consolation, we shall omit them at present in order to come to chapters 34 - 45, which is a whole section on one major theme. These twelve chapters focus on the theme of resisting the Word of God. As you settle down into the book of Jeremiah and read chapters 34 - 45, watch how the focus is repeatedly on resisting the Word of God.

This section brings us to the period of the disaster of 587 BC when the city of Jerusalem was burned and the last segment of Judah was taken into exile to Babylon.

Now let us look at our theme as it appears in chapters 37 - 39.

You can resist the Word and yet have keen interest in it

It is not that Zedekiah is irreligious — he is not. There is a semi-optimistic moment in the first part of chapter 37. It seemed as if Pharaoh's army had come from Egypt to the aid of Judah and Jerusalem, and so the Chaldeans, the Babylonians, who were besieging Jerusalem, withdrew because they were forced to go down south to deal with this Egyptian threat. Zedekiah and his advisers were beginning to think that their pro-Egyptian policy might be working and that Egypt might really come to their aid.

So at this possibly optimistic moment King Zedekiah sent word to Jeremiah saying, 'Please pray for us to Yahweh our God. We need a national day of prayer, Jeremiah.' That was his concern. He was no secularist. But you notice that Jeremiah's answer in 37:10 was, 'This is not going to work, Zedekiah. In fact, even if you defeated the Chaldeans, even if you reduced them to nothing but wounded men, those convalescent Chaldeans would rise up and burn Jerusalem.' So the word Zedekiah faces has not changed.

I want you to look here at Zedekiah's pattern and see how he approaches Jeremiah. Look at the little episode in chapter 37:17-21. Jeremiah had been thrown into prison, and in 37:17 King Zedekiah sent for him and questioned him secretly in his house and said, 'Is there any word from Yahweh?' Jeremiah said, 'There is. You shall be delivered into the hand of the King of Babylon.' That is how direct Jeremiah was.

But it is not as though Jeremiah did not have his own agenda. When he had the opportunity with Zedekiah he begged him in verses 18-20 to release him from the confinement of the dungeon lest he die there. He wanted to appeal to Zedekiah. He had a personal request to make and it is interesting that even though he had that personal request to make of Zedekiah he did not trim down the message or shape it or modify it. When Zedekiah asked whether there was any word from Yahweh Jeremiah said, 'Yes, there is. You shall be delivered into the hand of the King of Babylon.' So he did not modify the message at all.

But notice how much Zedekiah wanted to know. He sent for Jeremiah, questioned him secretly and conferred with him to discover the truth.

You will notice also that in chapter 38:14-28 Zedekiah reacted in the same way. This is after Jeremiah was raised and brought out of the cistern. Zedekiah sent for the prophet and received him at the third entrance of the temple of Yahweh. The king said to Jeremiah, 'I'll ask you a question. Hide nothing from me.' Jeremiah basically said, 'This is a hopeless case, Zedekiah. If I tell you, will you not surely put me to death? Even if I give you counsel you will not listen to me' (v. 15). He knows the king. It is not going to do any good. 'You want to know and ask and enquire what the Lord's Word is, but the truth is, it won't make any difference.'

He tells him the alternatives in verses 17-18. 'If you give yourselves up and surrender to the officials of the King of Babylon, your lives will be spared; this city will not be burned. If you do not surrender to the officials of Babylon, they will burn this city and you will be handed over to them.' Those are the alternatives; but this is a hopeless case because of Zedekiah's continual dithering.

You notice that even though Zedekiah vacillates and cannot make up his mind, he still always wants to know what Yahweh's Word is. He is always curious, he is always fascinated and always has to know. He is constantly calling Jeremiah in for private one-to-one conferences, but it will not make any difference. It is like somebody who is always checking the weather although it never makes any difference to him at all!

There is a humourist/satirist by the name of Garrison Keillor in the United States who has written several books. The setting for them is a place that he calls Lake Wobegon in Minnesota, up in the north where many Norwegians and Swedes have settled. They are a mix of Catholics and Lutherans and fundamentalist Brethren. Keillor talks in one of his accounts of the Tollerud family. Daryl Tollerud, who is in his 40s, works with his father on his father's farm. He is married and has a family and so is hoping that Dad will retire and hand the farm over to him. Apparently Daryl had real problems with his father, as others did, because his father hated making plans. On one occasion Daryl's father and mother had arranged a visit to Seattle. They were to go there on 30 June and plans had been made about seven or eight months previously. Then one evening the old fellow gets uneasy and says, 'I don't know about that trip to Seattle. I might be too busy. We'll have to see.' This is just the way he was, Keillor says. To agree to do something and have people expect you to do it bothered him. He could not bring himself to say, 'Tomorrow we shall do this' and stick to it. It was such insane dithering.

That is a picture of Zedekiah. He is just like a cartoon in Gary Larson's comic series called *Far Side* where he had a picture of what he called the boneless chicken ranch with chickens flopping around everywhere. That is the way Zedekiah was, and yet at the same time he had this interest, he had this apparent need to know what the Lord's Word was. So he would take the initiative and ask Jeremiah, but it would not matter. What do you do with a person like that? You can resist the Word yet have a keen interest in it.

There was another similar situation in the Old Testament years earlier, someone who was more hostile to the Word of God than Zedekiah — Ahab, King of Israel. You can read about it in 1 Kings 22. You may remember that Jehoshaphat, the king of Judah, had come north to meet with Ahab; and Ahab said, 'You know, Jehoshaphat, Ramoth-gilead, about twenty-four miles over there east of the Jordan River belongs to us. But we are sitting still and we're not taking it back from the King of Syria.'

Jehoshaphat responded, 'Well, I'm with you, but why don't we ask the clergy about it?' Ahab had his four hundred prophets. He asked them and they all voted in favour. But, although he does not say it in so many words, Jehoshaphat smelled a rat and said, 'These guys here all get their cheques from the court. You don't happen to have a real prophet of Yahweh here, do you?' Ahab replied, 'Well, there is one, but I hate him because he never prophesies good about me but always disaster, Micaiah the son of Imlah. But we will bring him in.'

So they brought him in and Ahab put the question to him: 'Micaiah, shall we go up to Ramoth-gilead or not?' Micaiah answered: 'Sure, go up. The Lord will give you success.' He said exactly the same as Ahab's paid prophets said. Ahab's response was, 'Micaiah, how many times must I go on putting you on oath [the Hebrew verb form is a participle, continuing action] to say nothing but the truth to me in the name of Yahweh?' (1 Kings 22:16).

What does that mean? It means that this had happened before. Who knows how many times? It was a game that Micaiah played with Ahab. Ahab brought him in and asked him and for all the difference it would have made, Micaiah could just have said, 'You know, the price of beef has gone up, Ahab.' It did not matter what the Word of the Lord was. It would not make any difference with Ahab. After that, Micaiah gave Ahab the 'revised version' — if he went against Ramoth-gilead, it would be the last thing he did (1 Kings 22:19-23, 28).

After Ahab had put Micaiah in prison he still went off to battle and told Jehoshaphat to put his royal robes on while he himself would be disguised as a private soldier. Now that is interesting. Why did he do that? Because he was afraid that Micaiah might be right — and he was.

There you have that contradiction. Ahab hates the Word, but he insists on having the Word. He will not follow the Word, yet he is fearful of the Word. You see the contradiction in man as a sinner? He can resist the Word and yet have a keen interest in it. But when that happens, the Word of God becomes a mere formality.

So that is where we are in chapter 38:15: 'If I give you counsel you won't listen to me. Though you want the Word it won't make any difference.'

In one of his books Richard Bewes tells of a time when he was leading a mission at Durham University. He met a cynical theologian who was also an atheist. Richard questioned him and said, 'Why theology?' His answer was, 'It amuses me.' Zedekiah was no better. So there is this strange perversity that you can be fascinated with the Word of God but will not follow it; or you can be fascinated with Jesus and what Jesus says: 'If anyone would come after me, let him deny himself and take up his cross daily and follow me' — but you will not do it. You can resist the Word, even though you have a keen interest in it.

You can resist the Word though you have reason to believe it

Jeremiah makes a dig at Zedekiah in chapter 37:19 at that first major interview. Jeremiah says to Zedekiah, 'Where are your prophets who prophesied to you, saying, "The king of Babylon will not come against you and against this land"?' It was a great one-liner. You can pick up allusions to such false assurances in some of the other texts in Jeremiah, for example 14:13, where you have the reference to other prophets who were prophesying that the Lord would give them assured peace in Jerusalem and Judah. In 23:16-17 you find prophets prophesying that no disaster would come upon them. You meet Hananiah in chapter 28 saying that within two years they would have Jehoiachin (the previous king) back and the vessels of the Lord's temple back. What happened to him? Well, soon he was six feet under.

'So where are your prophets, Zedekiah, who prophesied that the king of Babylon would not come against you? But he has!' You can resist the Word though you have reason to believe it. 'Zedekiah, the evidence is right in front of your face. The Babylonians are here as I said, and yet you are still refusing to believe the Word that comes to you through me.'

You can find the same kind of resistance to the gospel in our day. It is not because of a lack of evidence. Naturally, some may claim that there's no solid evidence for, say, the truth of the gospel story. They may say that they think that anything that smacks of religion is simply mystical and spooky and subjective and cannot be supported. But they should know better. They should face the four Gospels. I don't mean that they must take them as God-breathed, but they ought to acknowledge that they are purported historical documents that have the right to be regarded as credible unless there is clear evidence to the contrary. And what do those Gospels claim to be? The product of eyewitnesses. What you see in the Gospel accounts are things that these eyewitnesses, these believers in Jesus, told others when they were preaching the gospel in the land of Israel in the days after Jesus' death, resurrection and ascension.

What did they have to do? Well, in preaching Jesus, they would have to explain what he did and what he was like and what he said. They would speak about what they saw, heard and experienced. For instance, he raised Jairus' daughter, he brought her back to life, and he cast a legion of demons from the guy from Gadera. He had power over demons; he had power over death; he had power over disease; he forgave sins. Remember that episode in Mark 2:1-12 where four men came and pulled up the roof and let down their paralytic friend, and Jesus not only restored his health but forgave his sins; or at least you can say that he claimed to do so.

What does one make of all that? These were things that the early preachers of the gospel said and preached as eyewitnesses, as men who had been there. Here's the crucial point: when they were preaching these things, they were preaching to other eyewitnesses, and they were often preaching to a lot of *hostile* eyewitnesses. If what the preachers were saying was not true, those hostile eyewitnesses would have exposed it as a fraud in the first century and you would never have heard of Christianity. Why didn't that happen? Because even the hostile hearers could not dispute the truth and accuracy of what these original evangelists were proclaiming. When you preach in front of hostile hearers, you have to be careful with your facts. So, if you resist the gospel, do not claim that there is not enough evidence. There is evidence for you to deal with.

I was recently reminded of something C. S. Lewis wrote in *Surprised by Joy*. He related how in his atheist days he was impressed and somewhat disturbed by G. K. Chesterton's book, *The Everlasting Man*. But what really shook him was something that happened shortly after he had finished Chesterton's book. 'Early in 1926 the hardest boiled of all the atheists I ever knew sat in my room on the other side of the fire and remarked that the evidence for the historicity of the Gospels was really surprisingly good. "Rum thing," he went on. "All that stuff of Frazer's about the Dying God. Rum thing. It almost looks as if it had really happened once."' Lewis says that to understand the shattering impact of it you would certainly need to know the man, who had never shown any interest in Christianity. 'If he, the cynic of cynics, the toughest of toughs were not — as I would still have put it — "safe", where could I turn?' It disturbed him.

But, sadly, evidence did not disturb King Zedekiah overmuch. And you, too, may resist. You may think there is not much real evidence for the gospel and for its reliability. But have you really considered it? No, do not let anything disturb your citadel of unbelief. You can resist the Word, even though, as in Jeremiah's case with Zedekiah or in the case of the Gospel accounts, you have reason to believe.

You can resist the Word by submitting to fear

Now this is obvious with Zedekiah, but just let me point out how and where this takes place. You see something of the weakness and cringing outlook in 38:5 when some of Zedekiah's courtiers come to him and complain about Jeremiah. They claim that Jeremiah is undermining the morale of the people by what he is telling them. They need to be rid of Jeremiah.

In 38:5 Zedekiah says, 'Behold, he is in your hands. The king can do nothing against you. I just don't have the power to oppose you fellows.' He is a weakling. You see this of Zedekiah even more in the face of Jeremiah's promise and threat in 38:17-18. That is where Jeremiah once again laid out the alternatives for Zedekiah. He said, 'If you surrender to the king of Babylon, the city will not be burned with fire and your life will be spared. If you don't surrender, the city will be burned and you will not escape.' Zedekiah reacts by saying, 'I'm afraid of the Judeans who have deserted to the Chaldeans, lest I be handed over to them and they deal cruelly with me' (38:19). Derek Kidner in his commentary writes, 'O, my! What kind of a concern is that?' If you read the account of some of the conditions in this Babylonian siege of Jerusalem in Lamentations 4, Zedekiah should have had more concern for others. There were children wandering around desperately begging for food. There were mothers who had apparently cooked their own dead children in order to get some food. That was the situation; and yet

Zedekiah was only worried about what might happen to him if he surrendered.

So Jeremiah issued a clear demand in chapter 38:20: 'Obey now the voice of Yahweh in what I say to you.' That is the demand. But Zedekiah vacillated, dithered and became the royal ping-pong ball.

This leads us to something we need to formulate and put down as a principle. You can resist the Word of God, not because you are vicious but because you are weak; not because you are hostile but because you are fearful. You see a sample of that in John 12:42-43 in a New Testament setting: 'Nevertheless, many even of the authorities believed in him, but for fear of the Pharisees they did not confess it, so that they would not be put out of the synagogue; for they loved the glory that comes from man more than the glory that comes from God' (ESV). They were driven by fear.

Tragic consequences resulted because of what Zedekiah did not do on that dark day in 587 BC. Because the day came, chapter 39:4-7, when the Babylonians made a breach in the wall and entered the city; it was that night that Zedekiah and the contingent of soldiers around him fled (39:4). They attempted to leave by way of the king's garden through the gate between the two walls and escape towards the Jordan River. But the Chaldeans pursued them and overtook Zedekiah in the plains of Jericho. When they had taken him they brought him up to Nebuchadnezzar king of Babylon at Riblah in the land of Hamath and he passed sentence on him.

Riblah was sixty-five miles north-north-east of Damascus. That is where Nebuchadnezzar had his 'western' headquarters. They took Zedekiah and his contingent up there. What happened? King Nebuchadnezzar had the nobles of Judah slaughtered and then he slaughtered Zedekiah's sons before Zedekiah's own eyes. Then he commanded a Babylonian lackey to scoop out the eyes of

Zedekiah, clamp him in bronze fetters and cart him off to Babylon. What was the last thing that Zedekiah ever saw? He saw his own sons slaughtered in their blood because he had dithered and played around with the Word of God and forever worried and feared about what people would think or might do.

I think we can understand that Zedekiah was obviously submitting to fear. I think we need to understand also that most of us are fearful people as well, but that Jesus understands our fears. The Lord never mocks us for our fears, but he does tell us in Luke 12:4-5 that we have to prioritize our fears. He says, 'I tell you, my friends, do not fear those who kill the body and after that have nothing more that they can do. But I will warn you whom to fear: fear him who, after he has killed, has authority to cast into hell. Yes, I tell you, fear him!' (ESV). That is the fear that Jesus tells us we ought to have. All other fears are second-class fears. But if you are a Zedekiah clone, you will resist the Word by caving in to fear and by forever worrying about what other people are going to do to you or think of you.

Though many resist the Word, there will be a faithful remnant

The events in 38:7-13 and 39:15-18 will be our focus for this point. We are looking at Ebed-melech and what he did. Ebed-melech was concerned because Jeremiah had been thrown into the cistern (first part of chapter 38). So he went to King Zedekiah and appealed to him to allow Jeremiah to be taken out of the cistern, or he would die of hunger because there was no bread left in the city (38:9). Why would Ebed-melech imagine that Zedekiah would reverse his orders so soon after condemning Jeremiah to the cistern?

You have to know Zedekiah!! That might have been Monday when he allowed them to throw Jeremiah into the cistern. This was Thursday! I have an esteemed friend and he is really a very astute scholar, but he has admitted that he is 'a-mill' on Monday, Wednesday and Friday and he is 'pre-mill' on Tuesday, Thursday and Saturday and on Sunday he rests. That is a Zedekiah view of the last things!!

When Zedekiah gave him permission, he told Ebed-melech to take thirty men with him (38:10), probably because he might meet some resistance. We do not know what is going on in this court, but there were obviously some opposing forces and it was very likely that Ebed-melech would meet resistance over hauling Jeremiah out of the cistern. So he took a company of thirty men with him to do this, but Zedekiah had at least given him permission. Nevertheless, this placed Ebed-melech in danger from the king's advisers. This is reflected in 39:17, where the Lord refers to the men of whom Ebed-melech was afraid. There were men out to get Ebed-melech because he helped Jeremiah.

Now Yahweh gave Ebed-melech a special assurance through Jeremiah after he had been taken out of the cistern. But let us back up a moment: as soon as Ebed-melech was given permission to rescue Jeremiah, he went to the wardrobes where they kept old rags and cast-off clothes and grabbed a pile of them. He let those down by a rope to Jeremiah in the cistern. 'Jeremiah, put these rags and old clothes between your armpits and the ropes and then we will hoist you up.' And so they did.

The Lord does not forget such kindnesses. Matthew 10:42 says that the Lord does not forget cups of cold water given in his name — nor does he forget soft rags given in his name. So the Lord gave Ebed-melech a special assurance at the end of chapter 39: 'Behold, I will fulfil my words against this city for disaster and not for good... But I shall deliver you [Ebed-melech] on that day, declares Yahweh, and you shall not be given into the hand of the men of whom you are afraid; for I will surely save you and you shall not fall by the sword; but you shall have your life as a prize of war because you have put your trust in me, declares Yahweh.'

You see what is happening in chapters 37 - 39? There is a sense in which you have two people, polar opposites — just as you might say Adam and Christ are the two men at the end of Romans 5, so here in Jeremiah 37 - 39 you have Zedekiah and Ebed-melech. You have the one who is afraid to believe and the one who believes in spite of his fear. Ebed-melech receives this marvellous assurance from the Lord but he is the opposite number from Zedekiah.

The point about Ebed-melech is that he was a foreigner. He is called a Cushite (38:7), usually translated 'Ethiopian', but it may mean north Sudanese. He could have been from Sudan, there is a little debate on this point, but he was not an Israelite, not a Judean; he was not one of the covenant people; he was working as a slave in the king's household. His name, Ebed-melech, means 'slave of the king', so it may not have been his personal name. But there he was. He took his stand in faith beside Jeremiah despite his fear and came to the prophet's rescue. Jeremiah did not have any people standing beside him, but here was one man who did. Who knows what Ebed-melech's assistance and friendship and faith must have meant to God's servant Jeremiah? We could say that Ebed-melech is the Old Testament Onesiphorus. You may remember him from 2 Timothy 1:16-18, where Paul said, 'May the Lord grant mercy to the household of Onesiphorus, for he often refreshed me and was not ashamed of my chains, but when he arrived in Rome he searched for me earnestly and found me — May the Lord grant him to find mercy from the Lord on that Day!' (ESV). What impressed Paul? Other people were turning away from him; but here was one who was not ashamed of Paul the prisoner, was not ashamed of his chains; was not afraid to refresh him, give him help and minister to him, and even searched him out earnestly in order to take care of him and visit him.

That is what you have in Ebed-melech in Jeremiah's case. In the face of abandonment and faithlessness, the Lord in his kindness often does this. He provides someone to stand by your side as an assurance and encouragement in the midst of the darkness. The Lord himself still thinks of you, and sometimes that is all you may have; but sometimes he graciously gives you someone else who stands there with you.

In John Buchan's book *Witch Wood*, set in Scotland around 1644, there was a young village pastor, named David Sempill. He had run into some heavy weather and was probably going to be turned out of his charge by the presbytery, although not for any doctrinal heresy. He was undergoing quite a bit of conflict. There was a man called Amos Ritchie in his congregation. After church, on one of the last Lord's Days that David Sempill preached before his expulsion, Amos Ritchie was hanging back as if he wanted to talk to the pastor. So as he left the church Amos walked with him to the manse and talked as if he was having a hard time getting around to what he wanted to say. He talked about the weather and about crops. Then they got to the manse gate and Amos Ritchie said this: 'If there's deep waters to be crossed, sir, I'll ride the ford wi' ye.'

I know it is not historical; I know it is a novel. But can you imagine the impact that has, that there is someone willing to stand beside the Lord's servant in the mire?

There is a true illustration concerning William Still. When he commenced his pastorate in Aberdeen, he was a single man and his aunt served as his housekeeper. It was in the early days, I think, of that pastorate and Mr Still says that he felt impressed by the Lord to preach on judgement and hell. He knew as he kept preaching on such biblical texts that it was beginning to weary the people and press them down. That was the setting.

One Sunday, he and his aunt sat at lunch. Still says that the Word had been particularly hard that day; indeed, hell had been the topic for weeks. In their conversation his aunt spoke out: 'I'm sitting with them in the pew and taking it all. I feel for them. Oh, Willie, is there no love in the gospel?' That shook him, but he had to say that he could do nothing but what the Lord had lain on his heart. 'Well,' said Auntie, 'if it goes on there will soon be no one there but you and me.' 'And will you desert me then?' Willie asked. His aunt answered: 'Never. I committed myself to you and the Lord's work here and I will never leave you.' You could almost put those words in the mouth of the Saviour. In the midst of the darkness and the muck and the mire, sometimes you may not have an aunt to say that; but you have a Redeemer who would say it. 'I've committed myself to you here and I will never leave you.'

So it is pretty bleak. This is not a happy part of the book of Jeremiah at all. Jerusalem is burning in chapter 39. At the end of this segment, all we can see are two believers standing there — Jeremiah and Ebed-melech. But that is enough to support what the *Westminster Confession of Faith* says in chapter 25, section 5. It is a slice of the confession that speaks about the church and it states all kinds of qualifications. It says the church can be more or less pure; the church can have all sorts of problems in it; it can be more or less faithful. It even goes on to say that there are some churches that have so thrown out the gospel that they are not even true churches of Christ but are synagogues of Satan. Then in the last line of that section the confession says, 'Nevertheless [lovely word!], there shall be always a church on earth to worship God according to his will.'

That is true even in Jeremiah 39. Jeremiah 39 is not Acts 2, it is not the day of Pentecost, it is not an optimistic time; but there are two men still on their feet. There shall always be a church on earth to worship God according to his will. Though many resist the Word there will always be a faithful remnant. Jesus will build his church.

Faithful futility, a pattern of ministry

Jeremiah 40 - 45

Introduction

We are looking at 'faithful futility, a pattern of ministry', and this matter is broader than just preaching; it covers the waterfront of pastoral ministry. I have been fascinated with how Jeremiah could stay on his feet, given all he endured, and so I want to give some attention to these chapters which speak of the latter part of Jeremiah's days.

In the Market Garden offensive of World War II there were some British troops pinned down somewhere in the Netherlands. The Germans were shelling the British battalion headquarters. Apparently a Roman Catholic chaplain, Father Egan, went down into the cellar where the troops were trapped to find out what was happening to the wounded. He met Sergeant Jack Spratt (his real name!), who was renowned as the battalion comedian. Sergeant Spratt said, 'They're throwing everything at us but the kitchen stove!' He had barely said the words when the building suffered another direct hit and plaster and debris came showering down on them; and when they found their feet again, right in front of them was a kitchen stove! Spratt looked at it and said, in essence, 'I knew they were close but I didn't know they could hear us talking!'

Now, obviously, in ministry there is a certain degree of conflict, and there is a certain degree of hardness and of difficulty, all of which varies in intensity. Sometimes the circumstances of ministry become so dismal that you are almost convinced matters could not get any worse — but then they throw the kitchen stove at you. So when you begin to think that it cannot get any worse, the answer is, 'Oh yes, it can!'

That seemed to be the case for Jeremiah after the devastation of 587 BC and with the exile of the rest of the people. (I should say that I am using Jeremiah's prophetic ministry as a kind of model while recognizing that he is different from us in that he was a prophet who received direct divine revelation. Still, there is a good bit of overlap between Jeremiah and ourselves when we think of serving God in the ministry of the Word.) There had been an exile of the cream of the crop in 597, but in 587, after the Babylonians returned, wrecked and burned down Jerusalem, most of the remainder were taken away to Babylon. The leftovers, if we can speak of them in that way, remained in the land. But in Jeremiah 40 there seemed to be a hope of making the best of a sad situation for those left in the land. It looked as if there might be some reason to hope that they could eke out a living and enjoy a reasonable existence in Judah. Gedaliah was the Babylonian-appointed governor; a Jew, but Babylonian-appointed; and there were some Babylonian troops stationed there, so maybe there was a possibility of making life work, maybe there was a ray of hope. It is at this point that you see Jeremiah exercising what you might call a ministry of faithful futility.

Jeremiah 34 - 45 can be divided into two major sections. In chapters 34 - 39 events are outlined *before* the capture of Jerusalem, ending with a promise for Ebed-melech. In chapters 40 - 45 events are outlined *after* the capture of Jerusalem, ending with a promise for Baruch, Jeremiah's scribe. But throughout those two sections there is one clearly defined theme. As detailed in chapter four, it is the theme of resisting the Word of God; and that permeates the whole of the twelve chapters.

So a question hangs over this section — was it worth ministering in that kind of situation? With this in mind, it is important to examine what Jeremiah faced and what records Jeremiah left of his ministry during this period.

A pattern to ponder (chapter 40, especially verses 4-6)

The captain of the guard, a Babylonian, tells Jeremiah, 'You can do what you want. You can come with me. I'll look after you well. Come to Babylon with me. And if it seems wrong for you to do that, then don't come. You can settle wherever you want here in the land' (see 40:4).

In verse 6 we learn of Jeremiah's choice. He 'went to Gedaliah the son of Ahikam, at Mizpah, and lived with him among the people who were left in the land' (ESV). Why did he do that? You have a servant of the Word living among what you might call the dregs. In Jeremiah 24 the Lord had given Jeremiah a vision of two baskets of figs; one basket was full of good figs and one basket full of rotten figs. The exiles taken to Babylon in 597 BC were regarded as the good figs by the Lord and the bad figs were the ones who would be exiled in 587 BC. The ones that were left might be described as the dregs of the bad figs and yet Jeremiah opted to stay with them in the land in this very, very difficult situation.

In the same way, the Son of God did not look for personal advantage. Remember Philippians 2:6-7: 'He took no advantage of his equality with God. Instead he made himself nothing by assuming the form of a servant.' And there may be times when you have to make a hard decision and when you opt to make the non-attractive choice for Christ's sake and that of others, as Jeremiah did here. À la Philippians 2, we could call this Jeremiah's Jesus-decision. Sometimes that is the decision we need to make, sacrificing personal advantage and comfort and perhaps preference. There is a pattern to ponder here.

I was re-reading some of the missionary stories that Paul Long told in one of his books. He was a colleague in Reformed Seminary some years ago. He spoke of his time in the former Belgian Congo. There were a number of native preachers and evangelists, and one of them was Mutombo Elijah, who was regarded as the Billy Sunday or Billy Graham of the area. He was a very effective preacher and evangelist. But Mutombo Elijah contracted leprosy. Mutombo Elijah gave himself to prayer, asking the Lord to restore him. He went back in a week to the physician, who said, 'I'm sorry, Elijah, but you're going to have to go to the leper camp. There is no change.' So he went and his wife went with him. She said, 'Look, I'm your wife. I'm going to stay with you. If I and the children get leprosy, we'll take it as from the Lord, but I'm going with you.'

The leper camp was a place of thuggery, among other things. There was robbery, there were adulteries, and there was even murder. It was not a nice place and there was more than leprosy going on there. But there they began to work; and in the course of time a little church came into being. The church grew and finally, among all the churches in that presbytery, the leper church was the largest. Mutombo Elijah continued to labour there, but he never attended presbytery meetings because he was a leper. Some fifteen years later, all of a sudden, Mutombo Elijah turned up at presbytery. He was in his leper robes but he said, 'Brothers, I'm clean. God has answered my prayers.' Everyone was delighted. They said, 'Mutombo Elijah, we're parcelling out the churches for the next year and you can have your pick of any of the congregations you want to serve.' But he replied, 'You don't understand. God had to lay a very heavy hand on me fifteen years ago to accept this assignment to live and serve him in the leper camp. Without the leper's mark I would never have obeyed him. He's kept my wife and children clean; he's built up his church; he's answered much prayer. Brothers, God makes the assignments; he owns the churches. Who will take my place in the camp? Will one of you become pastor of the flock I serve? No, I will stay where God has placed me until he moves me out to serve another people.'

That is the decision Jeremiah made. He stayed in that bleak situation. That is a pattern to ponder. Now you notice that I described it as a pattern to ponder and not a strait-jacket to wear. I think we have to be careful here. The pattern is there (in Jeremiah 40) and is grounded in Philippians 2:6-7, but you can corrupt that pattern. You can 'perversify' it. Let's say you have the option of where you might minister and one possibility is appealing and attractive and one is difficult and torturous. Are you to assume that the more forbidding is always the Lord's will? Though I think I know better, that is my tendency. As if the Lord would never want me to have something that I might enjoy!

Now some of you perhaps might not understand that, but that is the way some of us think. It is similar to the Eliab situation in 1 Samuel 16 where the Lord says to Samuel, 'Don't look on his appearance or how tall he is because I've rejected him.' Well, you take that to the nth degree and you say, 'Well, if you want to serve the Lord, he only takes ugly people!' That is not a valid inference! So please understand — I am not trying to push this to the nth degree. The fact that Jeremiah chose to minister in a bleak and desolate situation does not mean that I am always called to do that. But there *is* a pattern I must ponder, and sometimes the servant of

Christ is called to set aside personal advantage and comfort in the ministry of the Word. Given what Jeremiah had been through, we may be at least surprised that he made that choice in this situation. It is as if he 'emptied himself'; he is a very Christ-like prophet. It is a pattern to ponder.

A tragedy to watch

This takes in chapters 40:7 - 44:30. What did Jeremiah face in his ministry at this point? At this point he faced a triple tragedy.

He faced, historically, a tragedy of treachery

You have this treachery in the rest of chapter 40 and in chapter 41. In 40:7-12 Gedaliah is setting up government and trying to establish some sort of normality. But there are problems. It looks as if life may be feasible in the land at this point for these 'leftovers'; but Gedaliah the governor is naïve (40:13-16); Johanan, one of the leaders of a military band, is devious (40:15); and Ishmael, the leader of another military band, is treacherous (41:1-3).

Johanan, a military leader who carried some clout, was talking to Gedaliah and said, 'Do you know that Ishmael is trying to kill you? The king of the Ammonites is behind him and he wants to eliminate you.' Gedaliah was naïve and said, 'Oh, no, no. I don't think so. I don't think that's right at all. I don't think that's fair to Ishmael...' (see 40:13-16). That was his attitude. Johanan was certainly no 'Mr Clean'. He had offered his 'solution' to Gedaliah: 'Look, Gedaliah, just let me take care of it. I could go and see that Ishmael was liquidated and nobody would be the wiser.' That is Johanan! It is devious; but at least he sees the true situation, while Gedaliah is gullible and later reaps the consequences. When Ishmael comes in 41:1-3 to visit Gedaliah, he and his ten men assassinate Gedaliah and wipe out the Babylonian troops who are there and slaughter many others. But Ishmael is finally driven off. Johanan takes over the leadership of the people that are left and they have to decide what to do. But there was a tragedy of treachery and now from the human perspective all that this little group can face is likely full and final Babylonian vengeance for what has occurred. There had been a faint gleam of hope, and then Ishmael and his thugs extinguished it.

This leads on to a tragedy of pretence

This is the second component of the tragedy in chapters 42 and 43. This group under Johanan makes an appeal to Jeremiah and they say, 'Look, we need the Lord's guidance on this, whether to stay in the land or flee to Egypt. Would you please pray to Yahweh and ask him what we ought to do so that we'll know.' Jeremiah responds: 'Yes, I'm willing to do that.' You notice in chapter 42:5-6 that they seem earnestly sincere and even go on oath saying, 'Even if what you say isn't what we want to hear, we'll do it.'

But their location gave the clue to their thinking, because in 41:17 they were down near Bethlehem, intending to go to Egypt. It was clear what they wanted the Lord's will to be. Jeremiah, though, asked the Lord and after about ten days the Lord gave him some revelation on the matter. His clear answer is given in 42:10-12: they were not to go to Egypt, for the Lord would grant them mercy in the sight of the king of Babylon and they would be safe if they remained in the land.

In 42:19, Jeremiah is very clear: 'Yahweh has said to you, O remnant of Judah, "Do not go to Egypt." Know for a certainty that I have warned you this day' (ESV alt.). But that was not the answer they expected. Kidner says they could not imagine that God's will was not in line with their own desires. For them, God's job was to offer approval, not to require submission. That was the attitude of these people. They basically said, 'No, no. That's not what the Lord told you. You got that from Baruch, your scribe. Baruch has it in for us. He wants us to get knocked off by the Babylonians. That's why you said that, so we're not going to follow what you said' (*cf.* 43:1-3). Do you see what their call to worship would be? 'Come, let us worship and bow down. Let us kneel before the Lord our puppet.' That was their attitude and that was the tragedy of pretence.

Then he faced the tragedy of defiance (chapter 44)

They do go to Egypt and here the defiance is even more blatant than before. Baruch and Jeremiah were forcibly taken to Egypt with this group under the authority of Johanan (43:6). So they went to Egypt with a group of ingrates and rebels and even there Yahweh had a word for these people through Jeremiah. Notice 44:8-10. Jeremiah, speaking for Yahweh, said to this group down in Egypt, 'Why do you provoke me to anger with the works of your hands, making offerings to other gods in the land of Egypt where you have come to live, so that you may be cut off and become a curse and a taunt among the nations of the earth...?' (ESV). That was a clear word. They were engaged in idolatry, worshipping other gods, even in the land of Egypt. Notice what a defiant response Jeremiah received in 44:16-17. They said to him, 'As for the word you've spoken to us in the name of Yahweh, we will not listen to you, but we will do everything we have vowed...' Even the women get in on the act in verse 19, telling Jeremiah that they did everything with their husbands' approval.

So this tragedy of defiance brings you to the very sad tragedy in 44:25. Jeremiah says to them, 'You and your wives have declared with your mouths, and you have fulfilled it with your hands, saying, "We will surely perform our vows that we have made, to make offerings to the queen of heaven…" Then confirm your vows and perform your vows!' That is the saddest tragedy!

You see what is happening? You see what Jeremiah told them? 'I hand you over to be the unending slaves of the bastard worship you crave.' That is the saddest tragedy: you persist in a path of ruin and God will allow you to enjoy your destruction. What Jeremiah did was to hand them over to what they so earnestly wanted to do.

In March 1945 some American troops ran into a German road block. The troops were from our 90th division and the company sustained some casualties. But they blasted away and wounded many of the Germans in the road block. The most seriously wounded was a young SS sergeant who was a real super-Nazi type. When the attack was over and they were treating people, this SS sergeant was bleeding copiously and needed plasma badly, and so a Captain Norris arranged to give this SS sergeant a transfusion. The wounded German spoke excellent English and demanded to know if there was any Jewish blood in the plasma. The medic had no idea. The German said he had to have a guarantee that there was no Jewish blood in the plasma he was receiving. Captain Norris had been listening to this. He went over to this SS sergeant and he told him in very positive terms that he did not care whether he lived or not; but that if he did not have the plasma he would surely die. Norris said, 'He looked at me very calmly and said, "I would rather die than have any Jewish blood in me." So he died.'

They handed him over to what he so earnestly wanted. That is what Jeremiah is doing in the last line of 44:25, and that is a tragedy. Sometimes you see that in ministry today. Sometimes you cannot be sure it is happening, sometimes you can.

You may think as you look at chapter 44 and at this second component of Jeremiah's experience that these defiant Judeans are going to face judgement for this; but you would be wrong. No, you are watching the judgement actually happening in chapter 44! The wrath of God is being revealed from heaven. You recall how Romans 1 teaches this? Three times you read: 'God handed them over...' God hands people over to what they refused to let go of — and that is the tragedy in Jeremiah's ministry.

A promise to hold (chapter 45)

Now this has to do with Baruch and the promise made to him. 'Thus says Yahweh, the God of Israel, to you, O Baruch. You said, "Woe is me! For Yahweh has added sorrow to my pain. I am weary with my groaning and I find no rest" ... Thus says Yahweh, "Behold, what I have built I am breaking down, and what I planted I am plucking up — that is, the whole land. And do you seek great things for yourself? Seek them not, for behold, I am bringing disaster upon all flesh, declares Yahweh, but I will give you your life as a prize of war in all places to which you may go"' (ESV alt.).

Now this is the promise to Baruch, just as there was a promise to Ebed-melech in chapter 39. But you notice in 45:3 that Baruch is sorrowful. The Scripture has had an effect on Baruch. Note that verses 1 and 3 refer to something that happened twenty years before in Jeremiah 36 (check the date given here in verse 1). It was about 605 BC, the reign of Jehoiakim, and Baruch had copied down a digest of Jeremiah's prophecies up to that point. He then took it to the temple to read it. Some of the godly officials in Judah thought the king needed to hear it. So they took the scroll and read it to the king. That is when Jehoiakim cut off three or four columns at a time and burned them in the fire. But when Baruch was taking down that record of Jeremiah's prophecies it affected him. It was not just a matter of, 'Oh, I'm a scribe — it's my job to write this down.' No, the content of the word he wrote down, of the judgement that was coming, agonized his soul. 'Woe is me! Yahweh has added sorrow to my pain. I'm weary of my groaning and I find no rest.' Who knows what precisely moved him; but in some way that message of judgement unsettled Baruch; it stirred him; it saddened him; it had a good effect on him in a way. He was not in neutral. He was grieving over what was coming on his people.

But the Lord said in 45:4, 'Baruch, you need to think a little bit about what this coming judgement means to me, not just what it means to you... Look at it from my perspective.' Then he so much as said, 'But you can't seek great things for yourself. You may not even enjoy a normal life, given the judgement that's coming; but I'm giving you a promise: I'll give you your life as a prize of war in all places to which you may go' (see v. 5).

So let us try to put this personal assurance given to Baruch together. Notice its position. The promise was given in 605 BC, but Baruch recorded it — or Jeremiah and Baruch recorded it — and placed it here in chapter 45, apparently after they arrived in Egypt in 585 BC (approximately). So in a situation twenty years after Baruch actually received that promise, he records it and makes a particular point to note it. What does that mean? He received the promise originally in 605; but at this time he was trudging into Egypt with a hostile group who, according to 43:3, did not think too much of Baruch anyway; and he was remembering the promise that the Lord would give him his life as a prize of war — and he had done just that so far. He had survived 587 BC when the Babylonians overran Jerusalem; and so far Baruch, for all his enemies and all Jeremiah's enemies, was still walking around alive.

In the face of fresh hostility against him, in the face of these refugees going to Egypt, he was still holding on to the promise of Yahweh, a God who could preserve his people in the face of trouble and danger. He was holding on to an old promise in a new situation.

Here's the question I want to raise: Is not Yahweh's keeping of Baruch a pointer to the way he always keeps his fragile, fearful, and hated people? Is not Baruch a representative of the remnant in Judah and of God's preserving of them? How precarious the situation of true believers in Judah must have been, as Baruch's was, and yet he was holding on to Yahweh's promise nevertheless.

We do not always realize how precarious things are. About two years ago, I read of an Englishman by the name of John Richards. He was about sixteen years old in 1948 when he fell out of an apple tree from which he was stealing fruit. He had some injuries. They treated him for a broken wrist, but that was it. But at the age of seventy-four, on a visit to his doctor, he found out that he broke his neck when he fell out of that apple tree and had fractured vertebrae as well. That is an amazing thing. He had just complained of some neck pain that he had had all those years. It seems that he had led a very active life, one time working on a farm, and then he had about fifteen years as an amateur boxer, in which any wrong punch could have killed him. How precarious that was! So they rushed him into surgery and put an inch-long bolt in his neck. But how fragile and how precarious life can be. This is especially so for God's people, who so often seem to teeter on the edge of extinction. It was that way for Baruch; that is frequently the way it is for Christ's battered flock. Obviously, the promise to Baruch was a promise of physical preservation, but I think it means even more.

I think Baruch here is, as I said, the embodiment of the remnant, and here is where I think the ministry so often finds its hope. For me, the doctrine of the remnant in Scripture gives hope to my ministry. I see it mostly in the Old Testament, but it is in the New Testament as well. Walk into Luke's Gospel and whom do you meet? Elizabeth and Zechariah and Anna and Simeon and Joseph and Mary; the remnant of Israel is there. God has kept his people.

That is so encouraging, especially if you minister in somewhat disappointing and discouraging circumstances. Again and again in the Old Testament the Lord preserves a remnant of his people. What hope that ought to give us! The church, too, has always recognized this hope in the doctrine of the remnant. There were the Waldensians in the Piedmont area of northern Italy. They were beaten up and hunted down, betrayed and butchered. But there is a *Waldensian Confession of Faith* and we sometimes use it in our worship service. The confession dates from 1655, I think. There is a statement in it about the church: 'We believe that this church cannot fail, nor be annihilated, but must endure for ever.' They found the hope in the remnant doctrine, in the remnant promise. *The Belgic Confession* (1561) expresses the same idea: 'This holy church is preserved by God against the fury of the whole world, although for a while it may look very small and as extinct in the eyes of man.' That gives me great hope. If I am called to minister among God's people and it seems utterly bleak, I still know that God is going to have a remnant and preserve it. So there is a promise to hold.

A question to face

Consider then the ministry of Jeremiah and Baruch. No king paid heed to the prophet's word. The people were carried off to Babylon and exile. Another fiasco occurred with the disaster to this rump people left in the land. Now they are heading to Egypt because no one would listen to the word of Yahweh through Jeremiah, and in Egypt Jeremiah speaks Yahweh's word faithfully, and still no one will listen. No one listens to him; he is carted off to Egypt, where he apparently dies. John Bright wrote this in 1965 about Jeremiah: 'He was, let it be admitted, as the world evaluates such things, a failure — a heroic failure, to be sure, but a failure nevertheless. His words were never at any time heeded; he could not, for all his efforts, deter his people from the suicidal course that he knew they were following. Nor was he a man who was able to achieve serenity, some triumphant inner peace, in the midst of the frustrations that beset him.'

Now, what is the use of a ministry like that? Well, among other things, does it not tell us (though I am not saying this is always the case) that service to Christ may prove continually agonizing and apparently fruitless? This should not surprise us particularly. Jeremiah's experience indicates that you have some situations in which you can serve Christ and meet nothing but hardship, trouble, anguish and frustration. If nothing else, seeing this may help correct the ministry-success syndrome that is so frequently beamed at us.

In *A Quest for Godliness* J. I. Packer refers to Richard Greenham, who was pastor in the late 1500s in a place about seven miles from Cambridge. He worked like a dog. He preached a sermon at daybreak four days a week to catch his flock before they went to the fields; he preached twice on Sunday; he catechized the children. He was known as a pastoral counsellor of unusual skill and even people from beyond his parish would seek him out. But what was interesting was that he seemed to have virtually no fruit among the people in his own congregation — his ministry there was virtually fruitless. He said, 'I perceive no good wrought by my ministry on any but one family.' Does that mean his work was useless? No, I think it just indicates that sometimes ministry can be apparently that fruitless.

So ministry can follow, I would hold, the same pattern as Christian discipleship in general. Look at Hebrews 11:32-40. That text tells us that we can really distort things by taking account of only one side of the evidence. When we look upon the believing life — or upon ministry — as consisting of conquering kingdoms, stopping the mouths of lions, quenching Babylonian fires, routing foreign armies and getting our dead folks restored to life (Heb. 11:32-35a), we forget that it may also involve torture, flogging, chains and saws, wandering around clothed in sheep- or goat-skins and trying to find shelter in holes and caves (Heb. 11:35b-38). Both sides of believing experience are there, and the writer of Hebrews is emphatic that *all* of them were 'commended by their faith' (11:39). It was not that some of them were deficient and that is why they did not get the goodies. No. These *all* were commended by their faith.

Back to Jeremiah and, as John Bright said, he was a heroic failure, but a failure nonetheless. The only adherents he seems to have touched are a few faithful government officials, an Ethiopian royal servant who knew how to use ropes and rags, and an upper-class fellow who attached himself to him as his scribe.

Now it is crucial to understand what this does *not* mean. If you see a ministry like that, what does it *not* mean? Leon Morris tells the story of a fellow, possibly in Australia, who was selling a house near a seaside resort. It was a beautiful home and had a lovely garden. He liked to use seaweed as fertiliser for his garden and it seemed to really work. But he had to move and he put his house up for sale and was very disappointed that no bids came in. Finally, it went to auction, and then he found out something. One of the people at the auction pointed to the seaweed on the garden and said, 'How often does the tide come up this far?' It was an unjustified inference. The inquirer needed to understand what this seaweed did *not* mean. It had been deliberately placed there by the owner.

So also with ministry that seems to be not very flamboyant and not very fruitful and not very successful — you need to understand what it may not mean. It does not mean that the smile of God is missing.

So faithfulness in futility is not useless if in so doing you are pleasing the Father. Then you are finishing well. You may go on meeting one failure after another, seeing no success in the Lord's cause, coming to the end of your days with a sense of abysmal disappointment, and yet finish well, because you have been doing the work he gave you to do, without much encouragement in it. Remember Bright's assessment of Jeremiah. He was a failure 'as the world evaluates such things'. So is it really futile? That is a question to face.

An anticlimactic observation

Now I confess that I may have a psychological attraction to the bleak side of matters. Nevertheless, I have found a view of Jeremiah's ministry almost a relief in contrast to the legion of proffered seminars, conferences, workshops and media hype designed to help me to a 'successful' ministry. There is such an earth-anchored realism in Jeremiah's ministry that seems so much more truthful than the razzle-dazzle often offered in our day. One final example: notice Jeremiah 20.

In Jeremiah 20 the prophet had just spent a night in the stocks, thanks to Pashhur, the chief of police in the temple. Then he complains to Yahweh. Jeremiah says basically that he is only given judgement to preach and gets mocked and ridiculed for it, and he wishes he could simply be quiet. But there seems to be such a thing as a fire burning in his heart (v. 9) that keeps him from being silent. Even in the face of personal danger he confesses that he has a defender (v. 11): 'Yahweh is at my side like a ruthless warrior.' So he seems to gather some hope and ends up by singing a doxology in verse 13: 'Sing to Yahweh, praise Yahweh, for he has delivered the soul of one in need from the clutches of evildoers' (New Jerusalem Bible). That is marvellous! We like that! We like to see things come out well. We do not mind distress and dismay as long as it only lasts seventeen and a half minutes with time for thirteen commercials and finishes up in the half-hour allotted with everything solved. We like to see prophets lifted out of despair and able to sing praise all within six or eight verses and we say, 'I thought that's how it works.'

But then Jeremiah plunges into cursing the day of his birth and cursing the poor fellow who brought his Dad the news of his birth! Look at verses 14-18: 'A curse on the day when I was born! May the day my mother bore me be unblessed! A curse on the man who brought my father the news, "A son, a boy has been born to you!" making him overjoyed...' (vv. 14-15, New Jerusalem Bible).

So maybe there were some scatterbrained editors of the book of Jeremiah who simply botched up the text here? No, I do not think so. My hunch is that Jeremiah and Baruch probably took care of the editing of this and they placed verses 14-18 right here after verses 12-13. It was no accident. It was as if to say, 'Do you realize that the transition from verse 13 to verses 14-18 is quick and easy and real?' In other words, it does not necessarily take long in the ministry to go from doxology to despair, from ecstasy to exhaustion, from confidence to cursing, from exulting in God to wishing you were dead. (So maybe we should not be worried about pride in the ministry, because despair may be just round the corner!) Whenever I teach or preach Jeremiah 20, I find that pastors have no difficulty at all in understanding the mood-switch between verse 13 and verse 14. They have been there. I guess it seems that I am ending on a bleak note, but it is not so much bleak as realistic. And not without hope! For what ministry can be hopeless if, like Jeremiah, we have Yahweh as a ruthless warrior standing beside us?